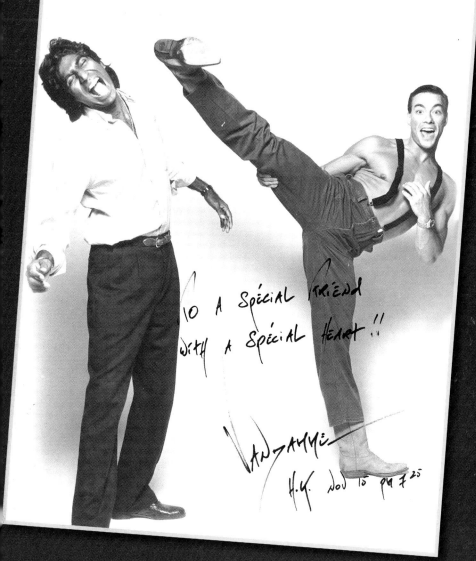

TO A SPECIAL FRIEND
WITH A SPECIAL HEART!!

VANDAMME
H.K. NOV 15 PM 7:25

ASHOK
AMRITRAJ
ADVANTAGE HOLLYWOOD

ASHOK AMRITRAJ

ADVANTAGE HOLLYWOOD

HarperCollins *Publishers* India

First published in India in 2013 by
HarperCollins *Publishers* India

Copyright © Ashok Amritraj 2013

ISBN: 978-93-5029-359-1

2 4 6 8 10 9 7 5 3 1

Ashok Amritraj asserts the moral right
to be identified as the author of this work.

HarperCollins *Publishers*
A-53, Sector 57, Noida, Uttar Pradesh 201301, India
77-85 Fulham Palace Road, London W6 8JB, United Kingdom
Hazelton Lanes, 55 Avenue Road, Suite 2900, Toronto, Ontario M5R 3L2
and 1995 Markham Road, Scarborough, Ontario M1B 5M8, Canada
25 Ryde Road, Pymble, Sydney, NSW 2073, Australia
31 View Road, Glenfield, Auckland 10, New Zealand
10 East 53rd Street, New York NY 10022, USA

Typeset in 12.5/16 Linden Hill by
R. Ajith Kumar

Printed and bound at
Thomson Press (India) Ltd

For my extraordinary parents, who I love and admire

For Chitra, my best friend, partner and wife

For Priya and Milan — you two are our proudest legacy and
greatest accomplishment

CONTENTS

KARMA

LIFE IS A MEDLEY of moods and choices. There are ups and downs and triumphs and failures. The most interesting moments are not the highs and lows but the turning points, the trembling moments of decision, of taking one direction and not the other. There are the tiny decisions – fish or pasta from the menu – and the life-changing ones. And I want to start my story with two of the latter sort.

I vividly remember the date. It was the 21st of February 1990, the day before my thirty-fourth birthday (gentle reader, don't bother to calculate, all that will come later) and I was restless, unable to sleep. I shan't say I was taking an inventory of my happy thirty-four years, but there I was contemplating the past and the future all at once.

I suppose an analyst – I don't have one and have never thought I needed one – may tell us how and why these decisions are taken but now, with the benefit of hindsight, I can see why I did it.

I had passed the night in that uncertain state between sleep and waking with a vague feeling of being alone, of being lonely. I waited for dawn and, inevitably, my parents called. It was the expected 'Happy Birthday' phone call.

I accepted their loving greetings and then said the six words my mother had been longing to hear: 'I am ready to get married.'

The words must have taken her by surprise. She had partially lost three sons to America and to American ways and tastes. There was a short silence. Was she thinking that I was about to announce my engagement to some American girlfriend? But if I had meant that, surely I wouldn't be relaying my readiness to her.

The Indian mum's instinct kicked in. I was asking her and the family to help me find a life companion. 'What is it you are looking for?' she asked.

I found, almost to my surprise, that I had the answer, a very precise one: 'A South Indian, Catholic and, of course, of the right age, educated, beautiful ...' and I added a few other qualities and specifications that occurred to me. I realized I had been thinking about it all night.

My parents were delighted, ecstatic. They said they would start putting the word out.

It was to be done in the age-old tradition of Indian arranged marriages with the concessions to modernity that I and any prospective bride of mine would expect. I knew that the first thing my mother would do was network by phone with relatives, near, dear and far, give them the news that Ashok was on the market so to speak, and did they know of any eligible girl of class and worth whose families could be approached. The relatives would then in turn put the word out to their near and dear, and the Catholic communities of Southern India would be alive to the fact that an eligible bachelor, one who lived in Los Angeles, had been a tennis player of renown and was now a Hollywood film producer, was looking for a bride. It would be the same if the bridegroom looking for a girl was an engineer, doctor, lawyer or businessman. In fact, I suppose, so unknown was the profession of 'Hollywood producer' that it might have, in some families, sounded a note of caution.

It would be the subject of more conversations than anything Jane Austen's characters could have dreamt of. And as I put the phone down, I realized that an Indian mother is a more effective mating agency than any fast-dating website or match-making service on the Internet. Yes, I had gone to the right place. But had I done the right thing?

By the date of that phone call I had spent almost fifteen years in the West. I had visited India and spent working and holiday periods there, but my 'home', or at any rate the house I called my own, was in Los Angeles. And yes, yes, yes, I had dated and had relationships with American girls or girls I met in America.

The last one, which ended a year before I made that phone call, was a serious involvement and friendship which had lasted years. She was some years older than me and an award-winning TV actor, very famous in her own right. I can honestly say that I learnt a lot from that relationship, about life and about what human beings want and get from each other. Yet it was not to be. The relationship couldn't lead to commitment for life, through no fault or trait of hers or mine and no great breach in what we had constructed over the years. It was just not my destiny, not what I would spend the rest of my life devoted to.

With my mother I told myself I had put out a feeler; I had not really taken the turn. Not yet! Yes there was no doubt they would find girls galore and present them to me and me to them and their families, but I could still say 'no'. It would disappoint my mother, but it wouldn't break her heart.

Still, the decision to ask her to find me an Indian bride was very firm. LA can be a very lonely place and over the months before my birthday there had been some changes. I had come to the US as part of a family with my two older brothers Anand and Vijay. We had for years been playing professional tennis and had at first been inseparable in work, play and mischief.

I remember that old 1950s' song by the Four Aces which goes like this:

Those wedding bells are breaking up
That old gang of mine.

There goes Jack, there goes Jim
Down to lovers' lane – (doo waak, doo waak!)
Now and then we meet again
But they don't seem the same

Gee, I get a lonesome feelin'
When I hear the church bells chime ...

Since my brothers had begun going steady with their future wives, a small breach had opened up in my existence. The eldest, Anand, had married and moved out to set up house in 1980, and a year and a half later Vijay got married. It had taken a full seven or eight years for me to feel the need to settle.

And then, informing that need was the pull of tradition. Loneliness and nostalgia are fast friends. This hankering for a life-companion was inextricably tied with being Indian, being South Indian, being Tamil, being Catholic and coming from the sort of family from which I came and which I missed. The assumptions, the comforts of a shared culture, the ambitions for the future and patterns of development of a family – all these were mixed in my plea to my mother.

Writing about it now has given me clarity. I can't say my

thoughts at the time were that specific or that I was aware that this was what I wanted, but yes, there was an emptiness to be filled. It's not that my days were empty. There was enough to keep me occupied. There were the regular tennis games, and there were parties and film premieres. And there was work. More of that later, but I had spent years knocking on doors creating opportunities which didn't exist to wedge my way into what seemed a very exclusive world.

I was producing low-budget films, some for the video market, some for the theatres, and one film paid for the next. But I hadn't yet broken into the world of the dream factory – the stories, sequences, sagas, myths, artistry and magic that had fascinated me and drawn me to Hollywood all those years ago during my boyhood in Chennai (then Madras) in South India. I was honest with myself, as so many beguiled by Hollywood are not. I was well within the networking circle of Los Angeles but I wasn't yet seated at the table and being dealt the cards for my next hand – I wasn't yet a 'player'.

I didn't in any sense underestimate the value and artistic merit of the work I was doing then or had done, and still count some of the films I produced at the time as among my favourites. When I made that crucial phone call home, I had just finished a movie called *Light in the Jungle*. It was based on the life of Albert Schweitzer, the musician who at thirty trained as a doctor and established a practice in the African bush. Malcolm McDowell, who had begun his career in Lindsay Anderson's legendary *If* and had then gone on to star in Stanley Kubrik's *A Clockwork Orange*, played the lead. Mrs Schweitzer was played by Susan Strasberg. They are both consummate actors. Nevertheless, I learned the elementary lesson that actors and directors don't always agree. And from my perspective as an Indian working in the Western genre I began to realize something else, something more profound.

The director of *Light in the Jungle*, Gray Hofmeyr, a South African, didn't always see eye to eye with the British-born-and-educated Malcolm McDowell. The film, set in a jungle village called Lambarene where Dr Schweitzer had built his primitive hospital, begins with Schweitzer digging the foundations for the construction. The script required that while digging he disturb the habitat of a frog. The director asked Malcolm to hold the frog that was supplied and smile at it. In an interview he gave later, Malcolm recalls the moment and the direction. 'What am I supposed to be smiling at?'

Whatever the director's reply, Malcolm said he wasn't doing that. There is a photograph of the young director squatting with his head in his hands at that moment. Gray wanted a sentimental moment, an expression of hope and courage as the missionary looked at the surviving creature. He couldn't convey this to Malcolm or if he did, the actor's instincts revolted against such sentimentality. I had grown up with both traditions, the stringency and subtext of some Western films and the sentimentality and melodrama of Indian films. I think I understood the clash.

The film turned out very well and Gray Hofmeyr won the Best Director prize at the following year's South African film festival. Roger Corman, veteran film producer, director and actor, known for his tireless, consistent drive, released the movie in the US in 1990 through his company New Horizons.

After the shoot in Africa, I had business to do at the Cannes Film Festival. Held in May each year, Cannes is one of, if not the most famous, film festival in the world. The Mediterranean town is a car's journey from Nice which is near the France-Monaco border. The festival takes place virtually on the waterfront. The good, the great, the not-so-good and not-so-great, the players, the hustlers, the stars and their entourages, the national associations representing every film-making, buying or exhibiting nation from the US to Upper Mongolia pitch their tents (literally) on the two-kilometre bay called the Croisette, or the crescent. There are yachts anchored in the bay and the Croisette along the marina is a necklace of grand, imposing hotels in which the stars and those on expense accounts take up residence for part of the week. For the last twenty-two years I have been a fixture at Cannes, and in the last decade my yacht parties and other events have been sought after by one and all. But more on that later.

The main business of the festival is the exhibition of new films and the judging of the coveted prizes – the Palm D'or for the best film of the year, the Camera D'or for the best film by a first-time director, the Jury prize and several others. The stars, directors and producers of the chosen films arrive in their limos and walk the red carpet through the crowds to the exhibition hall each afternoon and evening.

Not everyone goes to Cannes to see films. It's a market and an international meeting place. All day and into the night the terraces of the hotels and the tables of the restaurants which line the Croisette and the lanes that lead away from it buzz with the coming and going of people who have something to sell – a film, a script, an acting ability, an idea – looking for someone to buy. And the buyers come and cards are exchanged, deals sealed and further meetings scheduled, for the next day if it's urgent, or for London, New York or some other tall story if it's not. I actually did have business there that year. I had some finished films to sell and it was going okay.

I was seated at the Carlton Terrace one morning when a voice from across the crowded tables called my name.

A young man who looked familiar, but whom I couldn't immediately place, came winding his way through the tables to me with his arm raised in greeting. 'Do you remember me?'

'Yes, of course,' I lied, struggling to recall the place or circumstances under which we'd met.

Even the few words of introduction gave away his foreign-accented American English. Then he saved me the embarrassment of asking who he was. '1984. I sent you a letter. I sent 800 letters with my photographs and you were the only one who replied.'

'Jean Claude Van Damme,' I said, and he flashed his charming smile.

I remembered getting the manila envelope with the photograph and the letter. I was a young, inexperienced, out-of-work producer and I had invited the young man to come and see me. He did. He spoke only faltering accented English then.

'What do you do?' I had asked.

'I am an actor on the way to becoming a star,' he said. It was confidence, not conceit, and I felt it. Something told me the confidence would be rewarded, it would work out.

'Yes, but how do you live?' I asked.

'I drive limos,' he said, and smiled that winning smile.

Of course there was no way we could make a movie in 1984. I hadn't the finance and Jean Claude hadn't the English.

Now here we were in Cannes. He not only had the English, he had a deal with Stonebridge in which Michael Douglas was a partner.

We shook hands on it, agreeing to make a movie together.

We got back to LA and had to decide on a script. There wasn't one at hand but JC hit upon a story he wanted to do and he, Sheldon Lettich (the prospective director) and I began to develop it.

The story which we called *Double Impact* was set mainly in Hong Kong. Jean Claude plays the roles of twins who are separated at an early age and end up on different sides of wrong and right, of crime and the law. In the end, as with all conventional redemption stories, they join forces and fight for the right. *Double Impact* is an action thriller and is remarkable for the fact that the one actor playing the two roles differentiates them so brilliantly, altering his accents and emphases and making both – one who grows up in America and the other in an orphanage in Hong Kong – absolutely different and believable.

The shoot was quite complex because at the time the techniques for producing visual effects were not as sophisticated as they are today. We had to create the convincing effect of Jean Claude being two people and so worked with very early motion capture cameras. We had a dream crew to achieve this. Vic Armstrong, who had directed second unit on various James Bond films and on *Indiana Jones*, ran our second unit, and Richard Kline, twice Oscar-nominated Director of Photography, made great work of Hong Kong and its outlying islands.

At the same time, before the shoot, in the summer and fall of 1990, the serious work of bride-hunting had begun. I was in touch with my parents or, I should say, my mother was relentlessly in touch with me. She had taken my request to heart and so close to her heart that she saw it now as her mission in life. My poor father must have heard of nothing else, though he was a willing partner, if not a prime mover, in the quest.

They had put out feelers and had in the summer of 1990 gone around the world to make personal contact with the families

and girls they had been put in touch with, vetted and placed on
their long-list. They travelled to Singapore, Hong Kong (while
I was there on the shoot), Los Angeles, London and, of course,
various cities in India. The names, addresses, locations and mostly
descriptions of the status and educational qualifications of the
families that were sent to me made me realize how widespread
our community of South Indian Catholics was. A real diaspora
spread out from India stretched back generations.

My parents' search yielded a long-list of 300 families and girls.
In these affairs everything is managed with delicacy and decorum.
The enquiries are discreet and meetings take place between the
adult relatives of the prospective partners. This could entail 4–15
people meeting at the girl's house or in a restaurant to talk and probe
and get the measure and character of each others' families. By this
time photographs have been exchanged on which the mother and
other female relatives of the boy pass their opinions: 'rather too
dark-skinned ... hmmm ... very pretty/parrot/protruding nose ...
murderous eyebrows ... lovely hair ... too tall, too short/skinny/
rotund ... will she feed him/starve him/stuff him with unhealthy
rubbish ... ask for a full-length photograph so we can see if she has
child-bearing hips ...' and so critically, nit-pickingly on.

In some families (not ours) horoscopes are exchanged and the
stars consulted. The male members of the family also do a bit of
due diligence on skeletons in the family's cupboard – swindlers,
jailbirds, any case of bankruptcy and the like. In the event that
nothing comes of the meetings, no offence is given or taken. It's
all very civilized.

The process continued through the summer and finally my
parents drew up a shortlist. It was at this point that I was invited
into the proceedings and had to travel to catch glimpses and have

brief meetings with my prospective brides. The shortlist stretched to twenty (even the Oscars restrict themselves to ten in order to spare the jurors). I went to India, to Chennai and Mumbai, and then to Singapore and London and New York.

None of the girls worked out. It was clear my parents had chosen carefully and well and all the girls I was introduced to had everything to recommend them, but I was, without consciously telling myself, looking for that extra spark, that electricity I wanted to feel when some enchanted evening my eyes fell on that stranger across a crowded room. Romantic and exacting I suppose, but I needed that. Was I being too demanding? The question didn't, I must admit, trouble my conscience. Neither did the fact that my rejections and reluctance meant that my mother's quest would have to continue.

I had work to do – to get to Hong Kong and begin pre-production on *Double Impact*. By Christmas, after three and a half months, we were done. The schedule gave us a Christmas break before we went back in January to Valencia studios in LA to get on with the American end of the shoot.

My parents had taken account of the film schedule and had arranged for me to see seven more girls in Chennai during the Christmas and New Year break. I called my partners at Columbia Pictures and said I was off to India and would see them in LA after the break.

'To be with the family for Christmas, right?' was the obvious question.

'Of course. And ... er ... I want to get married next year and I'm going to meet my prospective bride.'

'That's wonderful, Ashok, how long have you known her?'

'I haven't met her yet,' I had to say.

CHITRA

SEVEN GIRLS, SEVEN VERY civilized meetings. That's the nature of the game – a carefully worked out informality. I thought long and hard about each of the girls I met and knew in my heart that thinking long and hard was futile. It wasn't there. My mother must have been disappointed and might have rued the day she produced a fussy youngest son, but she didn't show it.

On the Sunday before I was to leave for LA, the family went as usual to church. Our congregation gathers at the little church of St. Theresa of Avila in Nungambakkam, the part of Chennai where I was born and raised. The church was founded by Catholic officials of the East India Company and is dedicated to the sixteenth-century Spanish mystic and Carmelite nun. It has, in the style of Catholic churches in our part of the world, white-washed walls and wooden struts and roof, and always struck me as full of welcoming light.

That day as we emerged from mass my mother said, quite casually, 'I have one more girl for you to see.'

'Mom,' I said, 'I'm sorry. This is not working. I've run the course and it's probably me. I've lived too long in Los Angeles. I don't know what to say.'

I should thank God my mother knew what to say. She was

insistent. She said we must go to this girl's house. Her name was Chitranjali or Chitra and she was a famous sculptor's daughter. In fact, her grandfather too was a famous sculptor with commissioned works which stood as landmarks in our city and other cities of the South, and the family was very highly thought of. Her grandfather had been in the service of both British and South Indian royalty as an artist and had been given a title and land in appreciation. My mother added, as a coda, that things weren't perfect. The girl's mother was a Syrian Christian, so not of our religion, and her father was born a Hindu.

I consented so as not to disappoint or disobey my mother on the eve of my departure, and that afternoon we visited Chitra's home.

We were there for about an hour and Chitra was summoned but stationed herself at the other end of the sitting room from me, so I hardly got a chance to say anything to her. The conversation was all about what I was doing and what I intended to do and what she had accomplished at college.

As we left my mother turned to me, 'Well, what do you think?'

'She's lovely, but I didn't get a chance to talk to her. Perhaps you can ask her dad if I can take her out this evening,' I replied.

My mother thought about it for a moment. 'I'm not sure about that.'

But she did ring Chitra's father with this unusual request to allow his daughter on a date with someone she didn't know.

'Ashok's pretty well known, so they can't go anywhere public, but he can take her somewhere quiet,' was his very understanding reply.

It was a date. I picked her up at 6 o'clock that evening and we went to the beach. I say it was a date, but it was more like a film shoot because there were ten uncles and aunts who followed us, staying a hundred yards away but keeping a very close eye.

We found a spot on the beach to sit and talk and get acquainted. If not fascinated, I was gently intrigued by her. I later discovered that we were very near the spot where my mother and father had spent hours together in 1949 after they were engaged. I suggested to Chitra that we have a bite at Buharis on the beach, one of the famous restaurants of Chennai, again coincidentally where my parents had gone. Needless to say, we were followed there by the vigilante chaperones.

It was over two hours later that I dropped her and got home. My mother had been watching the clock. 'Well, is this it?' she asked as soon as I opened the door.

'Mom, I've spent just two hours with her. I have to go back to Los Angeles and think about it,' I said.

For the first time my mother demonstrated her disappointment and anxiety. She must have thought that at thirty-four I was getting a bit long in the tooth. 'You're never going to get married. You'll be on the shelf,' she declared.

I returned to LA and began the hectic shoot at Valencia Studios. On the third day after my return my mother rang.

'Well, have you made up your mind?'

'No, Mom, not yet,' I said, trying to think of some excuse.

'There are two other boys, NRIs (Non-Resident Indians – the phrase we use for people of Indian origin who are citizens of the UK, US or elsewhere) from America and England who have come to India looking for brides. They have both met Chitra and both want to marry her.'

I was speechless. It was an eventuality I hadn't considered. This was not just about me. It was about what Chitra wanted too. Boys? NRIs? How dare they? And they'd both made up their minds and made their offers? I spent a sleepless night. Was I dithering and missing the greatest opportunity life was offering me? The next morning I called my mother. 'Mom, I am seriously thinking about this, so please call Chitra and ask her not to reply to these guys right away, to put them on hold and I will make up my mind soon. We got on well together and I am sure she could wait a few days.'

Luckily, very luckily, Chitra agreed to put the two proposals on hold. I began to think, not of what I wanted but what she might want. I sent a message to her to say we should meet again and she should be kind enough to tolerate the fact that I had a shoot to finish, something that couldn't be abandoned, and that as soon as it was done I'd get to Chennai.

I did, and my mother invited Chitra over immediately afterwards and we spent another two hours together. The next day I was invited to her place and again we were given time to spend together. This was getting serious. The third day I asked her if she would come to the Connemara Hotel with me for dinner.

The truth is I couldn't stop thinking about her and every time I did, which was all the time, that excitement in the stomach overtook me. I had found out meanwhile that her name meant 'a pictorial offering', a tribute of beauty to the gods.

The Connemara was Chennai's smartest heritage hotel. The restaurant was vast, with art deco furniture, art nouveau-style chandeliers and a grand piano. The lighting was subdued for dinner. As we settled at our table and ordered, I discreetly conveyed a request to the pianist to play 'As time goes by', the eternal hit from one of my all-time favourite movies.

As he hit the first chords, I got up from my chair, fell on one knee and asked Chitra if she would marry me. As the waiters and other guests watched she was, to say the least, embarrassed and she quickly accepted my proposal, perhaps to get me off the floor.

We had known each other for a total of six or seven hours. I have often wondered what swept me along at that moment but can say with certainty that it wasn't the pressure of tradition. Though I had grown up in India, I had lived in Los Angeles for almost fifteen years and was very used to American ways. I had a house in Bel Air, had in my employ my great Indian cook and Man Friday and had a busy social life, and – to the extent I desired – a romantic life as well. But I knew with all my being that she was the one. Is that what being in love is?

Of course my decision also had to do with my mother. It was a tangled thought but I assured myself it was nothing to do with being mama's boy, which I am decidedly not. It had more to do with having absorbed the life and times of my father and mother and observing their tryst with happiness. No doubt their lives had ups and downs and my mother in spirit was the most individual human being I had encountered, but there was within her a vein of tradition, a dignity which came, I instinctively felt, from our culture. I was looking for it and felt I had found it. Chitranjali! There we were on the threshold of a life together.

This may be the wrong time to extol the virtues of an arranged marriage, what with our modern ideas of falling in love through a chance meeting or an Internet match. It is probably even the wrong time to assert that South Indian culture with its insistence that women are equal and mutual understanding is preferable, at least when looking for a wife, to the 'me, me, me!' subcultures that one can observe all around in Los Angeles. It is probably the wrong time to say that asking my parents to find me a wife was absolutely the right decision – and that is precisely the reason I have described it.

Needless to say, both families strongly supported our decision and there were huge celebrations all around. The news was conveyed to my brothers in LA and they sent their congratulations. They had been an integral part of the whole process and were elated at the news. Chitra's sister and brother-in-law live in Houston and they were told and they too joined in. After a heady week amongst her family and mine, I had to return to my film in LA.

I spoke to Chitra on the phone every day and all I can recall is her voice, her concerns, as I tried to explain the routines and the hectic schedule of getting the shoot done, going into post-production and meeting the tight deadlines that Columbia Pictures had set us. Sony was releasing *Double Impact* in August and both Jean Claude and I hoped and felt that this was going to be the breakthrough film for us. It would put us in places we had not yet been.

It took till June to deliver the film to the studio. We had to approve the trailer and artwork because those are the heart of the creative marketing campaign, the point of sale really, and one has to do two contradictory things with a trailer: to startle the audience with the unexpected and to appeal to their commercial and artistic comfort levels at the same time. In Hollywood you constantly hear the formula 'This is X (the name of a familiar movie) *meets* Y (another successful movie).' Producers and distributors want the elixir they know in new bottles, perhaps new cocktails.

So it was after we'd completed 'post' that I left for Chennai and Chitra in July.

I only had a week but we spent some wonderful times together. In the process I got to know her better. She had lived all her twenty-three years in her parents' home and, like many Indian girls of her class and of that time, had led a sheltered life. She had qualified as a lawyer and had practised for a couple of years, but I sensed that she was not really interested in being a legal professional and was biding her time.

We were in every sense betrothed and we now decided, after discussions with both families, that we would get formally engaged on 2 September and married on the 5th. That would give the relatives, and us, four clear days of celebrations, though in India festivities have a way of spreading out through more time.

We were to be married at San Thome Cathedral, the Basilica of St. Thomas the Apostle, in Chennai. It was where my parents had married, in 1949. San Thome has an interesting history. In the year of Our Lord, the first century AD, the territory which is now Chennai was a collection of villages. It is said that Thomas the Apostle (who has gone down in history as Doubting Thomas) landed on these eastern shores of India in 52 AD and began to preach the Gospel of Christ to the inhabitants of the coast. Twenty years later, while praying before a cross he was martyred, being speared in the back by those who denied and resented his ministry. He was buried on the rise around which the modern Chennai was later built, and which is still known as St. Thomas's Mount. A place of worship was built there by his Christian followers and in the seventeenth century, when Portuguese traders and would-be colonists arrived on the Coromandel Coast, they built the Basilica of St. Thomas near the sea front of Chennai where they had constructed an artificial harbour. The remains of St. Thomas were moved there.

San Thome is one of three sites in the world where the apostles of the Lord are consecrated, the other two being St. Peter's in Rome and St. Iago (James) in Spain. The church is whitewashed, with wooden beams inside, and used to contain the crypt where St. Thomas's remains lay. Today, these remains are in a neat annexe behind the Basilica, the ground floor of which houses a museum and precious Catholic relics of the saints.

Chitra, whose mother, as I have mentioned, was a Syrian Christian, was instructed in the Catholic faith by a priest at the bishop's house for a period of six weeks between my visit in July and our wedding in September and then was baptised. My parents became her godparents, a very important role in the Catholic tradition.

Back in LA, the premiere of *Double Impact* at the Westwood Mann Theatre was the grand affair that premieres and the parties that follow are. It was my first big premiere and I loved every minute of it. I knew that Hollywood was seeing me in a new light. Had I discovered Jean Claude or had he discovered me? Both of us had worked before but that letter six years earlier and that meeting at Cannes had started this fateful ball rolling. *Double Impact* opened at number 2 in the American box-office listings and in many countries in the world it had hit number 1. Its global performance exceeded all our expectations.

All the time I was thinking of Chitra and how my forthcoming marriage to a girl I had met for about ten hours in all would change my life. I knew that the festivities that awaited me would be more chaotic than the black ties, limousines, red carpets and congratulations that a film premiere entailed. I was bracing myself for the days to come.

From one carnival to another. The wedding arrangements had been taken care of by the time I returned to Chennai. Fifty friends from America and 200 relatives from various parts of India flew in for the five days of celebrations. I had never met many of the relatives before and I remember wondering whether my parents were sure that they were relatives, since we were putting them up!

Our house on Sterling Road, a 1940s' building with hints of colonial deco design, was decked with lights and there were flowers everywhere. The engagement ceremony began with the bride being decorated with patterns in mehndi on her hands and feet and ankles, executed with finesse by a professional artist. Then came the horse ceremony. The bridegroom is traditionally brought to the bride's home riding a horse and decked with vision-obstructing garlands of flowers from head to waist. The metaphor of the chivalrous knight in shining armour carrying away the princess is clear, but what's the curtain of flowers for? A hint that one is wandering into a future with a bit of beautified but limited vision?

My family was a trifle inept at hiring a horse. Instead of getting a tame one that was used to being marched through the streets with bands and drums blasting into his poor ears, they hired, through the family's network of contacts, a race horse with a pedigree. It was called Gray Grand and looked every inch its name. I was scared to death getting onto this beast that was used to the most professional jockeys on its back. It must have known I was an amateur because it began to resist the walk even as the procession of the 'boy's side' set out from Binny's Guest House where my relatives were lodged. It took four men to hang on to its reins as poor Gray Grand and I were led through the streets to the sound of the little orchestra of trumpets and drums that went before us and made a huge racket. The streets, with the cooperation of the Chennai Corporation and the police, were shut down for the passage of the *baraat* (the groom's procession) from Binny's to the Park Sheraton Hotel where my bride-to-be and her entourage awaited.

The traditions that most Christian families in India follow are very Indian, even Hindu, in origin though the dedication and vows remain Christian. The ceremony of arrival was followed by the engagement. Chitra looked stunning. With the pressure of having to do this, stand there, say that, I don't quite know how I managed it but we squeezed in a few games of tennis the next day with my American and British guests!

Then came the big day. Dressed in a sherwani I was driven down in a festooned car to the San Thome Cathedral. My brother Vijay was my best man. Chitra's father (as mentioned earlier a Hindu by birth and, I suspect, an agnostic by conviction) gave her away. Chitra was dressed in a sari and was, to my eyes and to those of the gathered well-wishers, a dignified vision. There was the Archbishop, bishops, monsignors and priests, a total of sixteen in all who served mass and presided over the magnificent marriage ceremony.

Chitranjali and I became wife and man. In keeping with my twin traditions I then changed into a suit and we went to the wedding reception. There were 7,000 guests including the chief minister of the state of Tamil Nadu, various ministers, and my good friends the Bollywood director Subhash Ghai and South Indian movie star Kamal Haasan. We had invited stars from the sports and film worlds of India, and a considerable contingent from both these worlds from abroad, people I had befriended during my career.

My hand ached with shaking and my arms with passing the gifts to the family members who stood patiently behind us and collected the presents. Chitra was overwhelmed, exhausted with it all. How do you write 'thank you' notes to 7,000 people? What do you do with thousands of gifts that very kind and thoughtful people think you'd need?

We went on a three-day honeymoon. Chitra and I were still getting acquainted. I told myself this was far better than the long-standing relationships that so many Western marriages are, in which a honeymoon is not an adventure of intimate discovery but a conventional, expensive, mostly unnecessary holiday. The film *The Householder*, made in the 1960s by Merchant-Ivory, comes to mind. A young Indian couple get married by traditional arrangement and the film traces their trajectory of subsequently falling in love. Marriage before love, but love follows – the ideal Indian way. Love leading to marriage – the ideal Western way. For Chitra and me it was an amalgam of the two.

From Chennai to Mumbai, where the showman of Bollywood Subhash Ghai held a star-studded reception and then on to Los Angeles as Mr and Mrs Amritraj in September 1991.

Double Impact was still working at box offices all around the world. I was a player! It was a good year ... okay, it was mind-blowing, life-changing ... I hate the word ... but it was definitely *awesome*.

PARENTAL GUIDANCE

BEING THE YOUNGEST OF three brothers, and till late adolescence clearly the most ungainly looking, the least accomplished and even clumsiest is, let me tell you, not easy. It can breed anxieties, but within the cocoon and shelter of a very caring, nurturing family it only spells competition and the urge to achieve, and not neurosis and disaster. At least that's my story.

An early picture can give you a clue. There we are, the three brothers in a row – Anand, perhaps seven years old, Vijay who was then five and I two. My brothers have smartly brushed hair with neat and possibly Bryl cream-ed partings. Their smiles reveal their confidence. And there I am with a dumpy frame and bunched, woolly feminine hair, dressed in a smock, with a happy but uncertain smile. What am I supposed to be?

My mother loved all her boys, but wanted the third child to be a girl. Unfortunately, that was not to be. I was born at the Isabella Nursing Home in Chennai in 1956. About ten years after India had gained its independence from British colonial rule, but the city into which I was born was largely a creation of the Raj. Most of the European nations were on their trading and colonizing adventures in the sixteenth and the seventeenth centuries and Chennai became a fulcrum of traffic and trade. In 1612 the Dutch established a trading post to the north of the city and then, in 1639, the British East India Company obtained a trading concession from the then Hindu kingdom and built a fortified settlement, Fort St. George which, in the next few hundred years, became the seed from which the modern city grew.

Our house on Sterling Road in Nungambakkam stands in the centre of this city in a by and large residential district about five miles from the extensive beaches bordering the Bay of Bengal. I call it our house but it's really an estate consisting of several buildings – some dating back to the nineteenth century – some outhouses and annexes within a large walled compound. In the 1940s my mother's family acquired the property and began building on it.

My mother was one of six children. Her father, Dr Dhairyam, was, unusually for his time, a distinguished psychiatrist. He was of the generation of Freud's disciples, and psychiatry and analysis were at the time new disciplines in Europe and much more so in India. For several years, my mother told me later, he worked at establishing the causes of epilepsy and looking for a cure. He died the year I was born and with his memory grew the legend in the family that had he lived he could quite possibly have made important discoveries in his chosen field and even won a Nobel Prize.

This mention is important only because it points to the fact that achievement and recognition were valued by the Dhairyam family. A prize was always good, something to be sought after, not for itself but for the fact that it marked excellence. This family attitude was certainly a spur to the competitiveness that made all three of us brothers tennis players of world calibre.

It was the same spirit that carried my mother through St. Agnes's College, an academy for girls run by Carmelite nuns, and then to Presidency College, and that impelled her to stand for and be elected the first lady chairman (we'd call it 'chair' now I suppose) of her college student union. It also assisted her in becoming this prestigious institute's captain of the tennis team. I believe the posters all around the city announcing the games billed her as 'Chairman of the College Union'. Did my grandfather exercise any influence over the wording of these posters?

My father was no less an achiever but was more laidback about success. He was born in a small town called Erode in the Salem district of Madras presidency as it was called during the British Raj.

He was also part of what would be considered a large family today but at the time was of average size. He was the sixth of six boys along with a sister. The second eldest brother was called Samuel, probably Samuelraj and somehow, perhaps through the agency of a literature-loving English teacher or headmaster, acquired the name Samuel Johnson.

Though born and brought up an Anglican, my father, I suspect, was not that informed about or into religion until he met my mother. The unspoken treaty in the house was that the religious education of the children would be the responsibility of my mother and the Dhairyam family.

Catholicism in India must date from the mission of St. Thomas to southern India and it was consolidated on a larger scale by the Portuguese trade and then the colonization of parts of India's west coast, notably Goa and the territories around Bombay (now Mumbai) and the east coast, where they built a basilica to the saint. In all the history of these conversions, which gives India its substantial minority Catholic population today, there is no account of coercion as there is in the history of the Conquistadores in

South America. Neither is there any record of friction between the majority Hindu population and the Catholics as there has been between Hindus and Muslims. It's not that there was no friction or resentment at all, but by and large mutual tolerance prevailed.

A network of British Anglican missionaries was established in India at the time. They ran churches for the Anglican community and did the very important work (as did the Roman Catholic orders which had existed in India for centuries) of running and teaching in schools and colleges. So strong is the tradition that people still refer to anyone who goes through an English-medium school and college as 'convent educated'.

My mother's family may have been very early converts but even the names, derived from Sanskrit, which they retained and traditionally passed down, reveal a comfortable and inclusive relationship with the culture of the country. We were and are very much Roman Catholics and very determinedly Indian. My grandmother and mother would celebrate such Hindu festivals as Dussehra and Diwali, participating in the ceremony of lighting oil lamps as a natural part of our culture while celebrating in traditional Catholic piety Christmas and Easter.

My father, whatever his beliefs, would be very supportive of our faith and the ceremonies that accompanied it. He would drive us to the Velankanni church of Our Lady of Health which used to be a six-hour journey to the south of Chennai. We'd start at five or six in the morning and be there for the mid-day mass and be back in Chennai by night. Today, with the growing prosperity of the region and the consequent build up of industrial traffic, the day trip has become impossible. I still visit Velankanni church with Chitra and my children on our family pilgrimage, but we fly part of the way and stay the night at the MGM resort at Velankanni which has grown tremendously in the last thirty years. (Ironically, the first studio in Hollywood I had a deal with was MGM, but that is a coincidence.)

My father, an English honours graduate, was a fantastic athlete through his student days and later competed in the high jump, long jump and hurdles and was also part of the university soccer team. Sport was, I guess, written into our genes. At college he did a lot of acting and singing and excelled at it, so much so that just before he was offered a teaching job, the well-known Tamil movie producer S.S. Vasan, who owned the famous Vasan Studios, presided over a dramatic function at my father's college and asked to meet him. He called my father over to his studio and was full of praise for his acting and singing abilities, and offered him a seven-year contract to star in his films. My father was tempted and may very well have gone into the acting profession. Fate and his brother intervened. They had other plans for him.

One of my father's brothers was Thangaraj and his wife Mary, my aunt, had a sister who worked at the time for the Dhairyams. She was Dr Dhairyam's assistant and close to the family as his clinic was run from rooms set aside in the family estate. My uncle and aunt knew that the one thing that any respectable family into which my father could perhaps marry wouldn't want was an actor for a son-in-law. At the time acting in movies was not really considered a respectable profession. They had passed broad hints to the Dhairyam family that their young and talented daughter who was finishing college was just the sort of bride my father could hope for.

My father was invited by Chairman Rao of the national Union Public Service Commission to come to Delhi and sit for the UPSC's qualifying exam. These were held once a year as an entrance to the prestigious government services including the Indian Administrative Service and the Indian Foreign Service. The Administrative Service was the successor to the Indian Civil Service of the British Raj which ran the empire for the British crown. It has a long and continuous tradition of service, expertise and even of adventure. Rudyard Kipling has made some of its officers in the revenue service, the railways, the builders and makers of the public works of British India, his heroes.

The exam was and is highly competitive. University graduates all over India took the exam and hoped to be amongst those who were chosen. My father did extremely well in the test and opted to work as an administrator in the Indian railways. Now this was a respectable job, one that any young man could socially be proud of and boast about.

In drawing upon my memory I recall the plot of the movie *Sliding Doors*. A woman wakes up and goes to work, passing through traffic, and boards a train to her destination. Her life takes on its routine. In a parallel story line we cut to her being stuck in a traffic jam. She misses the train, deciding in that instant to go back home before she takes the next train. At home she finds her husband, who has seen her off in the morning, in bed with another woman. Life changes.

I suppose everyone has wondered about the small decisions that lead to the big ones. There's a theory that the flap of a butterfly's wing disturbs the air ever so little but that disturbance combined with a multitude of disturbances contributes to a hurricane.

It's with this in mind that I recall that my father was first posted in a place called Perambore in his capacity as a railway officer and then asked to move to Sterling Road in Nungambakkam where the railways had living accommodations for officers. At the same time, the Dhairyams were moving from their house in a place called Kilpauk to their property on Sterling Road. This seemed to be a geographical assertion by fate.

My father was duly presented to the good doctor and his family and clearly remembers the first time he saw the girl who would be his future bride. She was perched on a stepladder, hanging a painting that had arrived from their old house. I imagine that on digesting the vision and then being presented to Dr Dhairyam and being asked some tough questions, Victorian-style, he must have thanked his stars that he hadn't taken up acting and had joined the railways instead.

After he had answered those questions to my future grandfather's satisfaction and proved that he would be a good match for the princess of the house, the families met to talk, to agree that this was the perfect match, to make arrangements and set the dates. The engagement ceremony would take place in December 1948 and the wedding would be a year later, on 29 December 1949.

The Dhairyam house wasn't too far from the apartments and hostels of the junior railway officers, my father's colleagues who would witness him trying to walk unobserved down the road. They knew where he was heading, that he was going courting, and he came in for a lot of good-natured cat-calls and whistles.

My mother was a willing fiancée but some time earlier, being a devoted Catholic educated by nuns, she had toyed with the idea of becoming a nun herself. She considered it for some time but decided, with more than a little help from her family, that she didn't have the ability for it. But she has remained devout all her life, dedicating herself instead to raising a family. I don't want to make it sound like that's all she did. She started her own business and made a success of it. She instilled in us the ambition and discipline that have carried each of us to where we are.

So my father did not become an actor and my mother didn't become a nun!

Their courtship was, for the times, a fairly liberal one. My parents tell me that they would be allowed out alone in the evenings to the terrace of the house where they had their trysts in the twilight air and then came to the Dhairyam's table when dinner was served. My father also recalls taking his fiancée to Buharis, earlier mentioned as the restaurant where, years later, I unknowingly took my intended bride.

Around the time my parents were married, India was not a happy place. The independence we won from the British in 1947 was clouded by the tragedy of the partition of the country into India and Pakistan. Large sections of the population, Hindu, Muslim and Sikh, were displaced and reportedly two million died in the carnage that accompanied this forced displacement of people from their country and their homes. The joyful feeling that great opportunities were opening up for once-colonized people was darkened by the suffering of partition.

In this ambivalent atmosphere my parents were married and settled into the Dhairyam household. Soon their first child Anand was born. He was followed by Vijay almost two years later and after another three years, in 1956, I came into the world – as Groucho Marx said, at an incredibly early age!

The British left us several legacies of their Raj and presence, not the least of which was that, apart from Tamil, we all spoke English at school and substantially at home. Chennai as I grew up was a British Indian city being slowly transformed. But the surviving institutions can still be seen today. There were British department stores like Spencers, Anglican schools, and the principal social forum of the British Indian city, the club – the Gymkhana Club, the Madras Club and, of course, the Madras Cricket Club. All around the city are monuments and buildings of British times, not the least of which are the old railway station and the railway building where my father worked and where my mother took us and which always bring back fond memories. There were the movie theatres and the coffee shops and needless to say the first films I saw were on the big screen because there were no small ones in those days. One cinema hall called Sapphire started as one storey in my youth and then became Chennai's first three-plex theatre.

The British also left us the tradition of fancy dress. There is a photograph of the three of us Amritraj brothers, with Anand looking very cool in a romantic cavalier costume, Vijay dressed as a grenadier and me as a short Roman soldier. The fancy dress or play costume which I remember best was given to me on my fifth birthday. Ironically, this birthday present was inspired by the creeping and lasting influence of America and American films on the world. It was a cowboy outfit and as I wore it and stood before the mirror I distinctly remember a new power flowing through me. My brothers at the ages of eight and ten were grown lads winning the admiration, I imagined, of all who gazed upon them. At last, with my hat and holster and flared trousers, I felt as confident. I could compete. It was a moment when looking in the mirror I could see myself in a larger world.

It was a tradition in our household to eat together at the dining table. On Sundays the cousins would gather at our grandparents' house while on week days we reverted to the nuclear family in our home above. My father would be at the head of the table. Grace would be said and the meal would commence with my mother assisting with the serving, parts of it fresh from the adjoining kitchen. When I was nine years old in 1965, we were sitting down to dinner and my mother left the table to fetch a dish she was warming on the kerosene stove. She must have turned after lifting the saucepan off the fire and somehow flashed the edge of the sari she was wearing over the flame. It was set alight and the flames quickly spread to the rest of her sari.

My mother appeared in the doorway on fire. My father leapt across the room and fell on her to smother the flames. I relive the horror of it to this day. My father managed to smother the flames but my mother was grievously burnt.

At the hospital they said it was touch and go. She had suffered 60 per cent burns. Many parts of her skin had been burnt away and the flames had gouged out parts of her flesh.

She was unconscious in the hospital for weeks and having managed to steer her through the symptoms of shock, the surgeons began their work on skin grafting. This form of surgery, perfected to a great degree as I write, was in the 1960s, and in India, in its very primitive stages but her surgeons at the Railway Hospital, Dr Cherian and Dr Govindaraj, were dedicated and determined. With improvisation and all the skills and resources they possessed they began the work of virtually restoring my mother's epidermis. It took her nine months of hospitalization to recover. My mother is a strong and determined woman and her will, I am convinced, assisted the expert medical attention she received in ensuring her survival and subsequent rehabilitation.

My grandmother took me very often, after school and on weekends, to visit her in hospital. And we prayed for her. We prayed by ourselves and we prayed to Our Lady of Health at the Velankanni church which is known as the Lourdes of the East as it is believed to have miraculous healing powers. Thousands of pilgrims belonging to various communities and castes flock here daily. The church has an imposing facade with tall spires and the wings are in the shape of a cross. In a niche in the altar is enshrined the statue of Our Lady of Health.

There are several stories about the origin of the belief attached to the church. One goes that fishermen at sea were caught in a dreadful storm off the Coromandel Coast and prayed to the Virgin Mary for their deliverance. She appeared to them in a vision, calming the waters and winds around their boat to see them safely to shore. Another story, from 1560, tells of the Virgin Mary appearing to a shepherd, asking him for milk to quench the thirst of baby Jesus. When the shepherd returned to his master, after performing the good deed, his pitcher kept filling up with milk. Consequently, a small thatched chapel was built at the site. At the end of the sixteenth century, the Virgin Mary appeared again in front of a lame boy who regained the use of his limbs. The church was constructed after the incident.

The tradition is to offer Our Lady of Health small gold and silver replicas of parts of the body in the shape of the ailment – a heart in case of cardiac complications, a liver in case of jaundice, lungs in case of tuberculosis and so on. We prayed, lit many candles and made offerings to Our Lady for the recovery of our mother.

She recovered slowly, went through rehabilitation, learning to walk again, falling many times, both inside our compound and later on Sterling Road. Her determination and great willpower are the qualities that inspire my writers and directors to create brilliant heroic characters. How great is it that I had such a character in my mother?

SHORT, FAT AND NEARLY BLIND

I MUST HAVE BEEN younger than five when I began school at the Presentation Convent in Church Park. It was a Roman Catholic school run by nuns, some European and some Indian. There were other teachers too as there are in most Christian educational institutions. Our uniform was white shorts, white shirt and, if I remember rightly, a tie. The uniform ironed out class distinctions between pupils. We were treated by the nuns as all God's creatures – some of us naughtier and less obedient than others.

At the age of five I followed my brothers to Don Bosco school, also a Roman Catholic school, run by Jesuit priests. The uniform there was khaki shorts and white shirt with a very prominent DB school badge. The school was a few miles away from our house and we'd be taken there every day by my mother in the car and she would fetch us in the evening. If she was otherwise occupied taking my brothers to their tennis coaching, I would be brought home by the house servant Baalan on his bicycle. He would heave my satchel on the handlebars, I would be placed on the grated pillion above the back wheel and off we'd go.

It may sound feudal now but Baalan and the other servants of the household were by no means menials. They were more the retainers of the family and some of them had been with us for years.

Though they had their place in the household hierarchy and took or sent their wages back to their families, mostly in the villages, they treated our house as their home and our family as, in a sense, their own.

Times have inevitably changed. Today's Indian household hires hands and labour as it needs them and there seems to be a very straightforward employer-employee relationship. Even so, in our household the old relationship between the family and the staff still persists. Raju and Murugesh, our household staff, have been with us about thirty-five years and are absolutely still a part of the family. This is our tradition and something created by my mother who commands the love and respect of the servants in a way no one else I know can.

One day, when my mother hadn't come in the car to pick me up and Baalan was for some reason late in arriving on his bicycle, I decided to make my own way home. I should have waited, but felt impatient and I suppose adventurous. I remembered the general direction and had observed the landmarks. What's more, I knew how to hire a rickshaw and did. But when my mother came to Don Bosco to fetch me and looked all over after most of the other pupils had gone, she was in a complete heart-pounding panic. She drove down the streets one way and the other, the household was put on alert and the servants cycled and ran down one side-street after the next near the home and the school, searching.

Unaware of all this I arrived home. I was standing next to my uncle Christy when she came in. She was obviously both very relieved to see me there and furious at me for causing them so much anxiety. She walked up to me and slapped me. It was the only time my mother has ever hit any one of the three of us. Immediately Christy put his arm around me and said, 'Maggie, stop it!'

It stung but I understood it. I realized how much my mother loved me, and today with kids of my own, I understand it even more.

I started playing tennis when I was seven years old. My brothers were already in training when my mother decided I should begin by picking up balls and throwing them back to the players. I was delighted. I knew it was a prestigious activity in the family.

Both my parents had been athletes, terrific athletes, my father in soccer and track sports. The tennis came from my mother's side. She had played tennis and represented Presidency College, Chennai, in the inter-university tournaments. She was among the first few Indian women ever to take up the vigorous sport. I can see her now as she must have been in her tennis kit which consisted of churidars and kurta.

It was great to be introduced into the family's tennis-oriented disciplines, but I soon learned that it was hard work. I remember my days being really packed. My brothers and I would wake up in the morning, change into our shorts and t-shirts and before we went for our run, we would have three raw eggs beaten with milk, perhaps one of the most foul things one could swallow, but part of our training for tennis.

We'd start off running down Sterling Road, which was much quieter than it is today, with very little traffic. It was a four- or five-mile run and my mother had set the course and trusted us not to skive, but to push ourselves to the limit of our stamina. We'd pass the residential end of Sterling Road and then emerge at the end where a bridge crossed the Cooum River that runs through Chennai. There were shops lining that part of the street at a landmark roundabout and, most famously, a bakery and the CVK Brothers' cake shop. That was where we would turn around, and then head back home over the bridge.

Our run became a noted feature of the neighbourhood. The early risers, the tradesmen and neighbours would see us go past, regular as clockwork. The traders, shopkeepers, the baker knew us and, from their comments and encouragement, regarded us as the young athletes of the city and later, of our country. There was in that era a special feeling about the place and a pride in our part of town. Chennai has expanded to perhaps ten times its size since and things have changed. For one, the baker's shop is gone.

We would return home sweating, panting, holding our sides, ready for a shower, breakfast and school. The run was always hard work and there were a couple of times when the three of us, some distance from the house, agreed that the full four miles was a bit onerous and that we should walk along and before the full course was run, sprinkle water on our heads, foreheads and necks to simulate sweat before we got home. We were not good frauds and my mother caught us at it one day. She insisted on following us in her car the next day!

That was a small deviation. The three of us really did work hard at being fit. The early rising, the run, school and our mum picking us up became the daily routine but that was just the start of the day. It was after school that the actual tennis training began. We'd be taken to a set of courts called Island Grounds. Our coach was a tennis professional called Rama Rao and he put us through our paces. We soon became his prize players. Rama Rao was a great coach. He was tall, thin, with straight black hair and aquiline features. He was soft-spoken but strict. He would, to start with, give me ten minutes of his time each session, throwing the ball to me to hit.

One of the other boys who would turn up for tennis training at Island Grounds under coach Rama Rao was Mani Ratnam who has gone on to become one of India's most celebrated film directors. He recalls today that when the 'Amritraj boys' turned up, Mr Rama Rao would clear the courts and his coaching schedule for them (us) while the rest of the trainees took second place.

We would practise for a couple of hours and then it was back home to dinner and homework before bed. We trained hard and I thank my mother with all my heart for pushing us. My grandfather had always said to her that he wanted someone in the family to play at Wimbledon and if it wasn't going to be his children then it would have to be his grandchildren. My mother must have kept that in her sights as the ultimate ambition.

She had by this time, along with a partner, started a business with the Rs 9,000 that her brother Christie, who passed away in 1963, had left her. The firm was named Magchand Industries, a combination of the partners' abbreviated names and it manufactured corrugated cardboard boxes. Packaging was new to India. When you bought vegetables or street food these were given to you wrapped in old newspaper. But the country was progressing and packaging became imperative. My mother was a brilliant and pioneering businesswoman and spotted that opportunity and potential for future growth.

From the first monies she made out of the factory, she bought each of us our first tennis rackets. She also taught each of us to drive a car in her spare time. The factory was started in the garage of our house and over the years expanded and became a flourishing enterprise. Our mother was an extraordinary woman of amazing energy – running a business, supervising us at work and play, cooking and then to crown the day, sitting down with the family at dinner. Today, I feel that much of my business acumen, foresight and passion I inherited from her.

Dinner in our household was a family affair. The evening meal was a time to discuss the day's events. Our parents always encouraged us to listen and participate in the conversation. The adults would talk among themselves and we would pick up this and that titbit until we were asked a question or invited into the conversation. Needless to say, with three sons at the table who were famished, the food disappeared fast and one had to be quick, but well-behaved.

On most days the conversation from our side was mundane – what happened at school or what happened at tennis. But at that age I thought it was wonderful. The spirit of being together, a family, some of us more equal than others, was really energizing. I looked forward to it each night.

At the time my mother's business was going well. One night at the dinner table I had my first lesson in business transactions. We knew the cardboard boxes, the product, would be transported by train to cities all over India. That night my mother was telling my father that a particular customer who owed her a decent sum for an order, which she had now dispatched by train from the railway station, had issued a cheque which her bank had just told her had bounced.

This set off a train of images in my mind. I didn't quite know what a cheque was but this piece of paper had been introduced into the conversation and I could, in my mind's eye, see it bouncing along. But where was it going? I paid close attention. My father thought for a moment. The order had been dispatched by rail? Yes! So it was on its way in a freight train from the railway goods depot? It must be! So then there's no problem, said my father. He was the Deputy Chief Operating Officer of Southern Railways in India. He could and would stop the train and get the order off it.

Before the boxes got to their destination, they were, on my
dad's orders, unloaded. The customer was informed and very soon
a fresh cheque arrived, was cashed and the boxes went their way.
It was old-fashioned leverage but I am sure my mother was glad
in this instance to possess it. It was one of the lessons I learnt and
it brings to mind the verse of the Tamil poet Thiruvalluvar:

To listen, learn and realize
The truth from whatever source
Is the mark of the wise

Some four decades later, that lesson served me well during certain
difficult negotiations on my films.

When I was ten years old, my brothers and I used to go to the
Sterling Club, the railway officers' club where my father was a
member. This was just down the road from our house. It had a
tennis court where we played at times, but it also had table tennis
tables and a badminton court and we got pretty good at these too.
We would go and meet friends there and go to the bar to drink
fresh lemonade after a sweaty game or two.

These officers' clubs are inherited from the British Raj and were
among the facilities provided to the armed forces, the railways and
the police who also had their allocated living quarters and 'colonies'
and compounds – sets of apartments or rows of bungalows. Apart
from these there were the gymkhanas and clubs of the civil servants
and professionals of the British Raj, now the exclusive territory of
those who consider themselves the Indian elite.

The gymkhana in Chennai was founded in 1884 and was at the
time exclusively for the city's white elite, though a few chosen
Indians were also granted membership. It is a splendid building

of the British Regency period with classical columns, a dance hall with a wooden floor leading to a 'buttery', the term still used in Oxford and Cambridge for a cafeteria. It has a swimming pool and extensive lawns and a large concrete movie screen for outdoor viewing. In 2009 I was honoured to be invited by the club president to give the Christmas message and many of my films have been screened there.

As teenagers we would go to the gymkhana on New Year's eve. The revellers, the 'society' families of Chennai, would turn up in their splendour complete with flashy jewellery. The gathering would have a fair number of teenage girls. There would be drinking and dinner and dancing to a live band. The convention was that the men approached the ladies and asked them for a dance. It was the era of ballroom dancing, rock and roll and jiving.

One had to summon the courage to ask girls to dance, simultaneously feigning a casual attitude to disguise the enthusiasm and the quickening of the heartbeat. Needless to say, the girls were watched closely by their parents and even though one longed for the slow numbers and the dimming of the lights, very few of us dared to do more than hold our dancing partners lightly by the waist and at a respectable distance. The young men who didn't soon got the reputation of being shameless, dangerous and even out of bounds to the girls of 'decent' families. On one occasion, a particular rogue was suspected of fiddling with bra-straps and buckles as he danced and he was declared persona non grata, and we defending cousins took to glaring at him to let him know that his crime against chivalry hadn't gone unnoticed!

It was at these clubs that we swam and played tennis, table tennis, badminton and other games from the age of ten onwards. Vijay would have been thirteen and Anand fifteen at the time.

Anand's concerns had begun to turn to those of adolescence – I mean girls! He was very successful in that department, especially in his later teenage years and on. I was oblivious, not envious, of it all.

Vijay had shot up in height and was already six feet tall. I inherited my height, or lack of it, from the Dhairyam family. In other words I was short and dumpy. Comparisons with my brothers were not at all flattering. My teeth always stuck out and my height and appearance, I thought and fretted, were not confidence-inspiring.

The final blow to my confidence was yet to come. I was driving with my mom and dad one day and my father asked me if I had noticed or read a particular billboard we passed.

I said, 'What are you talking about?'

He slowed the car down, pointed and said, 'There, read that.' He was testing my reading and probably my understanding of some smart advertisement.

I couldn't read it. The billboard itself was a blur.

At first, my parents thought I was having a bit of fun. It was a large billboard. 'I really can't see if anything is written on it,' I said.

My mother held my face in her hands and looked into my eyes. She knew what the matter was and close up to her face I could see the deep frown.

They took me to the ophthalmologist the next day and he tested my vision. I could read only the top of the eye-testing chart, the largest letters. We discovered I was seriously short-sighted and must have been from an earlier age, but had through the years accepted that what I saw was what everyone else saw.

It was not so. The doctor pronounced the numbers and my parents looked at each other. The myopia, the short sight began at -5.

At the time there were no correctives to short sight and I had to wear thick spectacles for which I was measured – frames that fitted my nine-year-old face. My eyesight deteriorated further. By the time I was fourteen and visiting London for the first time, my number was -9.5. Today I wear contacts and if I take them off I can't identify people in the room.

From the age of nine, I played tennis wearing thick glasses. Equipped with them my game must have improved and the world seemed so much sharper – harsher even. At school I no longer needed to sit in the first row of the classroom to read the board or to recognize which teacher was standing before us.

I was already so conscious of my physical appearance which was unflatteringly contrasted with that of my tall and good-looking brothers. I was a short, fat kid with protruding teeth and now thick spectacles. I got called names at school and elsewhere, everything from 'four eyes' to 'yelly' which is Tamil for a rat or a mouse. It caused me a lot of anguish and my mother who knew what I was going through was moved to tears. But even though I was insecure about the constant comparison with my brothers, I remained close to them and admired their every move.

This insecurity manifested itself in several ways. Air-sickness – chronic, bad, debilitating air-sickness – was one which stayed with me into adulthood. I could never trace the immediate cause. Was it the smell of the aircraft? I would go to a corner of the cabin or to the toilet and keep throwing up.

When I was sixteen years old, on my first tennis trip abroad to London, I went through a nightmare of a journey. I can recall getting there and still being sick, lying on a bench at Heathrow airport, waiting for the dizziness to subside and allow me to walk. The first-aid ambulance was called and they had to give me oxygen.

On an earlier trip to London we had stayed with my uncle. He had introduced us to an ophthalmologist who fitted me with my first set of contact lenses. At the time contacts were a fairly new invention and I was to have some adventures with them. But being able to do without my thick specs was a great boost to my self-image.

If I look at changes in my life, that was a turning point in my view of myself, in my confidence, and I resolved to tolerate the initial pain that wearing these primitively designed contact lenses gave me. After a while the pain abated. The next year I grew about eight inches. When one is happy, one's metabolism knows it.

BROTHERS TAKE ON THE WORLD

AROUND THE TIME OF my early visits to London, the global perception of India was quite different from what it is today. India then was not regarded as a tiger economy or an important world capital. Quite the contrary. We were seen as a vast, impoverished, overpopulated country, and a permanent part of the third world. Apart from poverty in the streets and the frequent reports in the newspapers of famine, drought and hardship, there were other signs of what the world referred to as 'underdevelopment'.

There were virtually no imports as these would be a drain on the economy, so chocolates, perfumes, whiskey and Parker pens were available only at exorbitant prices in the black market, brought in by smugglers. There were restrictions on travelling abroad – not a political denial of passports, but a restriction on the amount of money one could carry out of the country. No country in the world wanted to exchange their currency for Indian rupees, so all travel abroad was controlled by the Reserve Bank of India which allocated a meagre amount of foreign exchange, be it dollar, pounds sterling or rouble – though I don't suppose that there was an overwhelming demand for the latter at the time.

What Indians did in those days was buy foreign exchange in the black market, paying outrageous rates to dealers. My parents, though, weren't the sort to tolerate or even contemplate any sort of illegality, so the alternative was to travel without much money and rely on living with relatives like my mother's brother and wife in London or close family friends who had settled or earned money abroad.

For that first trip my parents had worked out how we could travel and pay for twelve days and see something of the world.

From London we went to Paris and stayed at the guest house of the Catholic Sisters of the Poor, a charitable organization that provides food and shelter to the sick and elderly and has branches in many parts of the world, including Chennai. For the past two decades, it has been a pleasure for me to support the great work they do. Today, when I stay at the George Cinq in Paris, I think about those days and even get nostalgic about them, trudging about the beautiful city and uncovering its mysteries and beauties through sheer leg power and the occasional and thrilling ride on the metro which went under the ground and ran along the streets mounted on stilts – something that Indian trains weren't built to do.

In Paris I also saw for the first time, going down the Champs Élysées, a boulevard with silver and golden lights coming one way and a stream of red lights speeding away the other – two-way traffic forming ribbons of light. We visited all the art galleries and saw the paintings we had only heard of. As we came out of one of the Paris galleries we were accosted by a photographer who asked if he could take our picture and who, without waiting for my father's answer, began clicking away. He had an Instamatic camera and asked my father, 'Do you want this picture?' My parents said, 'Of course!' not realizing that he meant, 'Do you want to buy this picture?' Having handed over the photograph he asked for the equivalent of $40, which in 1971 was not just a rip-off, it was an outrage. But my parents, being very South Indian, reserved and embarrassed about it and perhaps feeling a little foolish at having fallen for it, felt there was no way they could give the photograph back and refuse to pay. So they, unbelievably to me today, paid the $40. We put it down to experience and didn't let it spoil our trip.

We then went to a place called Noordwijk, a small seaside town in Holland where Anand and Vijay had some friends, and had played at tennis events before. The town is a delightful resort south of Amsterdam. The friends invited my parents and me to their place at 8 p.m., and we automatically assumed that they had invited us for dinner. It was cultural confusion. How were we to know that in the Netherlands it was customary to have dinner at 6.30 p.m.? Our anticipation soon turned into the realization that we had been invited for drinks and camaraderie. No food. We were left starving for the rest of the night.

Finally, and most significantly, we went to Lourdes where they immersed us in holy water, sunk us under in a second baptism. The water was ice cold. In a childhood baptism they pour water on the head of the baby while here they push the head into a large, ancient bowl made of stone. Only one's shirt gets wet, not the full body.

That trip was the first window to a real world which I now realize would have been much more bewildering if I hadn't had that other window to the world – the world of the moving picture which had given me glimpses of snow and mountains, foreign lands, languages – a universe removed from mine. The big screen was my passport to the secret garden, the rabbit hole that would take me to Wonderland. Was I obsessed with films even then? Why else would I have watched *The Sound of Music* thirty-four times?

Through all those thirty-four times I wouldn't in my wildest dreams have imagined that one day I would meet Robert Wise, the director of the film, who had also directed the classic *West Side Story*. I didn't just meet him by chance. We were introduced and became good friends while we both served on the Board for Foreign Films at the Academy of Motion Pictures. The first thing I said to him when we met was that I had seen *The Sound of Music* over and over again in Chennai when I was a boy.

'So that's where all that Indian box office came from!' he had exclaimed.

He told me he was genuinely astounded at the worldwide success of the film. He had ventured into it because he was a great fan of the music of Rodgers and Hammerstein. He hadn't set out to hit or play on the universal chord that the movie decidedly struck. He also said he made it very much so as to cast Julie Andrews and use her charisma and talent to construct one of the most remembered characters in film. But 'the casting of the girls just came together, like magic. I can't take the credit. Some other hand was at work.'

Julie Andrews often talked about the opening scene on top of the hill. The shot was taken from a helicopter with a very powerful wind-drag coming off its top propeller. The wind current was so strong that as the helicopter came in close to take the shot, she kept being blown off her feet and off the hill. I didn't ask how they finally got the shot. I assume they used a powerful long-distance lens. Anyway, the scene looks quite natural, like it's the breeze on that hilltop that's blowing her clothes.

I got to know Julie as well because I partnered on a film with her husband Blake Edwards who had made a great hit with the Pink Panther films starring the late Peter Sellers. In 2009 we planned the remake of his movie 10 that had been a huge success in 1979 with Dudley Moore and Julie Andrews and the discovery of global sensation Bo Derek. However, before we could get it made, sadly in December 2010, at the age of eighty-eight, Blake succumbed to a bout of pneumonia.

~~∽◈∾~~

That strange and wonderful world of cinema was initially revealed to me through the Sapphire theatre in Chennai. English and American movies were quite popular and from the age of seven or eight I began to acquire a taste for them. In between tennis and school work, I would go to the cinema. I saw Charlton Heston in *Ben Hur*, Sidney Poitier in *To Sir, With Love* and *Guess Who's Coming to Dinner*. Later on I saw Dustin Hoffman in *The Graduate*, and Sean Connery and Roger Moore in the James Bond movies.

Did I bunk school to sneak off to the cinema? You bet! It was always a gamble, but it paid off. That's partly how I managed to see *The Sound of Music* the number of times I did. Little did I know then that I would meet these icons of cinema, the people who had aroused these childhood obsessions of mine, and that our paths would cross, as friends, colleagues and partners 35–40 years later.

At that point in my life, Hollywood was a dream. At the end of some of the movies there would be a legend which said, 'When you're in Southern California, visit Universal Studios.' I longed to and in some recess of my mind knew that I wanted to, if ever I was able, be a part of the movie-making world. I think most children have imagined themselves as a character in their most loved film, or wondered what the life of a movie star would be like, but I always imagined what it would feel like to *create* one of those films.

~~∽◈∾~~

London, on my first trip abroad, left a lasting impression on me. What struck me immediately was the sense of order, the cleanliness. There even seemed to be a discipline to the noise. I am sure my memory has idealized the trip, but it felt then as if everything worked – the phones, the elevators, the lights, the machine that made tea, the taxis, the buses, the traffic on the roads, the clocks on the towers.

Most fascinating was the trip to Wimbledon – its grass court, the formal pomp and splendour underwritten by British modesty. No sense of flash – just dignified, confident superiority. It was called the All England Lawn Tennis and Croquet Club at that time and had the feel of a country club while at the same time being the arena for the most prestigious tennis event in the world. Anand and Vijay were playing in the tournament, so it was even more exciting. Watching my brothers play gave me a shot in the arm. I had to go back and work harder at my tennis so I could bring my skills to these courts.

I was in my final year of school by then and had been given an exemption, as my brothers had before me, to play in the Stanley Cup which was only for college or post-school students. Every college tennis player in South India plays in that tournament which takes place at Loyola College which happens to be across the road from our house.

My mother was watching me play in the finals and biting her nails as I played the best of five sets because my contact lenses kept filling up with dust and my eyes began to water, causing the contacts to drop and interrupt the game while I picked them up off the court. I washed them out each time, put them back on and continued playing. That was for me a memorable match. My opponent in the final was the reigning champion Vinoo Abraham and I won after a long and hard fought match.

So my last year in school was erratic. I must confess, if it needs saying at all, that I was probably one of the worst students amongst the thirty-five in my class. In the placing by grades I was constantly in the last five. The teachers didn't know quite what to make of my projected tennis career and of all the time that I was giving to it with my parents' consent. They knew where proficiency in Maths would lead, but where was tennis going to take me? It wasn't a profession at the time. There was only one real star tennis player in India prior to us Amritraj brothers: Ramanathan Krishnan. Even in international tennis, professionalism was just beginning.

As far as my teachers were concerned, they were comfortable with fellows who played cricket or hockey and went on to work in a bank or joined the army and played for the regiment's team or for the bank's recreational side. It was not something you did for a living. Parallel to their bewilderment was the fact that I was bringing accolades to the school. I had won the Stanley Cup for Don Bosco. Everybody was proud.

It was a paradox because this didn't insulate me from punishment. One of our teachers, Mr Selvadorai, who taught geography, used to exercise a peculiar method. If you got an answer wrong or if you were deemed to have been cheeky or been guilty of some other misdemeanour, he would pinch your ear between the nails of his forefinger and thumb and pull you painfully out of your seat. I was subjected to the procedure several times and still bear the scars on my ears. I could never master the names of the various mountain ranges that emanate from the Pamir Knot in south Central Asia, from which the Himalayas fan out.

There was on the one hand the indignity of being hauled up in this manner and on the other being something of a hero and celebrity for winning tennis matches. I don't know if that's being a good or bad student, but for better or worse that's what I was. And as Mark Twain said: 'I have never let schooling interfere with my education.'

It was in the autumn of my final year at school that I was chosen to be on the Indian National Junior Team which was to go abroad the next year. We were first put through two weeks of training in Patiala, a town located in the state of Punjab in northern India. There were four of us in the team and other promising players who attended as auxiliaries, and a gentleman named Akhtar Ali who was our coach at the camp for two weeks. It was, for a boy from the warm climate of South India, a freezing November.

We players were accommodated in the servants' quarters of the Patiala palace while Akthar Ali was grandly accommodated in the main palace. These servants' quarters had open windows, just rectangular holes in the wall with no grille or shutters. In those days we used to travel with 'bedding' – rolls of blankets, sheets and pillows in a canvas wrapping case that we called a 'hold-all'. It was unrolled on the floor and we slept in it. We would be woken up at 5.30 in the morning. A man would come and knock on the door and serve us tea. By the time he'd walked the distance from the palace kitchens to the servant's quarters, the tea was at best lukewarm. The lavatory, Indian style, was a hundred metres away across open fields. For me it was baptism by fire. Nevertheless, at the end of the two weeks we were extremely fit and ready to take on the world.

From the training camp I went straight to college to do what they called a 'pre-university' year in the Arts subjects. By that time

I was ranked number 1 in the country in the Juniors under-18 and I was to represent India at Wimbledon the following year. Before that, the Junior team was required to play all round the country in the national tournaments.

Even as I left school it appeared to be written in the stars, and quite firmly in my determination, that tennis was to be my vocation. It was my destiny. Most adolescents in India follow their fathers or close relatives into a profession or a business. For my brothers and me, tennis was the family business. The trajectory of that career was being traced out. My studies became secondary though I kept at them. I could always plead that I didn't do too well at school or college because the game took up all of my time and concentration, but the truth is I was not terribly clever. My daughter and son who are extremely gifted academically seem to have bypassed their father's genes!

Like all good Indian boys I did pass my school exams and went on to Loyola College, another Jesuit institution. Again my focus was not on my Arts course but on tennis, and the college was supportive and encouraging.

The All India Lawn Tennis Association was run by a Mr R.K. Khanna. As with a lot of enterprises in India, his son now runs it. Mr Khanna was not – how shall I put it? – a great fan of ours. He believed, with some justification, that too much power was concentrated in one tennis-playing family. It wasn't that Khanna was a tennis player. He was an official and had some power of patronage because he moved in government circles. To be honest, even at the time I assessed him as being an egocentric individual. He hated the fact that if we didn't show up for a tournament, the tournament became unsuccessful. It wouldn't be the same if the Amritraj brothers didn't agree to play. The public and audiences on the other hand loved us and rooted for our success.

In 1973 Vijay had an amazing year of tennis. He won his first international tournament in Bretton Woods in New Hampshire, US, and won a Volvo car along with his prize money. He beat Jimmy Connors and this was, naturally, big news in the international tennis world and very much bigger in India.

In the same year I went to Tehran to participate in the Asian Junior Tennis tournaments. The Shah of Iran was trying in every way to bring his country onto the international stage. I paid no attention to world politics at the time. I knew who the president of the United States was and I had read reports about the Vietnam War, I knew a little about the Soviet Union, but Iran to most Indians was unfamiliar territory.

What I saw on that visit was that Tehran had a veneer of modernity with new avenues and buildings, no restrictions on women's attire, night clubs where alcohol was permitted, and taxi drivers who spoke a smattering of English and who asked you what form of entertainment you were seeking. But beneath that surface there was brewing, though I saw no signs of it and was not in any sense politically equipped to see, the dissatisfaction that would lead to the Islamic revolution six years later.

Though it wasn't any milestone in the annals of tennis, for me, winning the singles and the doubles for India at the Asian Juniors was, at the age of seventeen, a hugely triumphant moment. It meant that my course was set. It had to be Wimbledon next and it was.

In 1974 I got my chance. I was selected to be on the National Junior Team and as the best junior in India, was chosen to represent India in the Juniors at Wimbledon. This was when I had my first real taste of premier class tennis. To my absolute delight, I found I was not playing beyond my league. I could more than cope.

I reached the finals of this prestigious event – only the second Indian to have done so at that time. Anand and Vijay reached the semi-finals of the doubles, and Vijay lost a nail-biting fifth set in the singles quarterfinals. Our names were everywhere in the press, both internationally and of course in India.

In the finals of the Wimbledon Juniors, I lost to Billy Martin who went on to become a world-class player and now coaches the University of California Los Angeles'(UCLA) tennis team. Living in the same city today, it turns out that his son and my daughter had played tennis a few years ago. At the end of their game his wife came up to my wife and said, 'You know, my husband knows your husband.' Chitra asked, 'How?' and was told that many years before they had played in the finals of the Wimbledon Juniors, and that her husband's name was Billy Martin! Billy and I then got in touch and went out and played golf together.

My brothers and I played at Wimbledon throughout the 1970s. The international press may have seen us as an unusually gifted family but the Indian newspapers adopted us as their darlings, their champions and heroes. We were photographed, written about, interviewed. Our past records were noted and our futures speculated about. I don't believe there had ever been three brothers playing Wimbledon in the same year before or since.

Each year, our parents made the trip to watch us play – the family was a team. It occurred to each of us that we had fulfilled our grandfather's dream. He would have been happy if just one of us had reached Wimbledon's courts. He must have been looking down from wherever he was and been triply proud.

CALIFORNIA DREAMING

IN 1975, WHEN I first landed in California, I was full of awe and amazement. It was, to me, magical. In the 1970s, America was the centre of the universe. It was, in every political and social sense, a continuation of the 1960s in which the world had seen the flowering and the tragic events and ultimate success of the Civil Rights movement, the beginning of a new generational philosophy whose art form pop had its high point in Woodstock. There was the promise of change, of wealth, and of love replacing the bitter war fought in Vietnam. In all this and the movement for greater democratic rights, with the Berkeley and UCLA campuses in the forefront, California was indeed the 'golden state'.

Was it real? Beverly Hills, the palm trees, the extraordinary weather and beaches with beautiful girls in bikinis all made up an atmosphere of make-believe. Like the Beach Boys said:

I've been all around this great big world
And I've seen all kinds of girls
Yeah, but I couldn't wait to get back to the States
Back to the cutest girls in the world
I wish they all could be California girls

In Hollywood, film-makers like Coppola, Bogdanovich and Roman Polanski had made their mark, though Polanski had fled to France under legal threat of prosecution for a socially unacceptable crime. But the gap was soon filled, and spectacularly, when film-makers such as George Lucas and Steven Spielberg were to come on the scene.

India was a place far away and the only thing that America knew of India was from the Beatles, Ravi Shankar, Maharishi Mahesh Yogi, and perhaps the Bleeding Madras t-shirts. Most Americans could not find India, let alone Chennai, on the map.

I have, earlier in the book, talked about life-changing moments. Well, this was one of those moments. As soon as I set foot in California and visited the studios, I knew that this was the place I wanted to live in, and this was the industry I wanted to be a part of, and be a success in. This is what I wanted to do, but tennis was the family business, and somehow I had to make that transition.

I had, as I said, heard of the studios and seen the ads at the end of movies inviting one to visit them, but I had never thought I'd be doing it. It was like being taken behind the drapes of a stage by a mesmerizing magician and being shown, to some degree, without the secret being completely revealed, how the trick was done.

I took cabs and drove around to the studios. There they were: Warner Bros, 20th Century Fox, Walt Disney Studios and Columbia Pictures. It was for me unbelievable and here I was, believing it! At Universal, I took the guided tour and felt I was identifying more of the sets and props and memorabilia than the rest of the group in my tour batch.

How was I to remain or make a life here? I knew nothing about films or the industry. I was a tennis player and that was my only profession. Could I use that expertise, that positioning in the world to make the transition to where I now wanted to be? The answer, as several years of wishing, dreaming and hard work proved, was 'yes'!

Tennis has always been an individual sport. All the professional tournaments like Wimbledon, the US Open and the French Open, as well as the other events, give primary importance to singles with the doubles and mixed doubles being attended when there are no great singles matches being played. The only team event in tennis at the time was the Davis Cup, where generally a four-member team represented an individual country.

For the first time in the United States, as with other US sports like football, basketball or baseball, Billie Jean King and her husband Larry King decided to start a tennis league which they called World Team Tennis. It started in 1974 and continues to this day, but its extraordinary success was between 1975 and 1980.

Vijay and Anand were already playing in the US in 1974, and in 1975 they were signed to play for the San Diego Friars, which was a team owned by Jerry Buss and Frank Marianni, a couple of successful real estate mavericks and very passionate about the game of tennis. They knew about me, the third brother, who had shown great promise at Wimbledon the previous year and gone on to play extremely well the rest of the year. So when Vijay suggested to Jerry that he bring me out to San Diego as a member of the San Diego Friars, Jerry agreed and flew me out from London in the summer of 1975.

My brothers and I stayed in a condominium at Solana Beach, a wonderful development very close to the Pacific Ocean. We were in training, and getting ready to play our first season of World Team Tennis – all three brothers on the same team. It was a wonderful time, and our parents visited us for a couple of months or more at our condominium.

In 1976 I was signed to play for Los Angeles, along with my brother Vijay and a top US Davis Cup player called Bob Lutz. Each team had three men and three women, and it was a total of five sets, the winning team having the aggregate number of games in the five sets.

We played at the fabulous Forum, and my journey and association with the entertainment industry really started. It was a time of meteoric rise for the game of tennis. Television and sponsorships had started coming in, and tennis had gone professional. The Association of Tennis Professionals (ATP) had been formed a few years earlier and we were a part of it, as were Connors, Borg, Nastase and all the other great tennis players of the era. However, there was only one family of three brothers that had ever played on the professional tennis tour, and once again, (the press and the public had not seen tennis players out of India) we were an absolute novelty, and extremely popular.

In the summer of 1976, playing for Los Angeles I got to meet many of my childhood heroes who enjoyed tennis: Sidney Poitier, Charlton Heston, Dustin Hoffman, Michael Douglas, Arnold Schwarzenegger, Buzz Aldrin (the astronaut), and many, many others. Between 1976 and 1980, when I finally made that fateful decision to enter the motion picture industry, I knew I needed to network, to develop these contacts so that I could make the transition. Tennis was the perfect platform to meet and engage with and, in some cases, learn from these iconic Hollywood figures.

In 1976 and 1977 we continued to play – after the World Team Tennis season that lasted about eight weeks, in the individual events all around the world. My parents would visit us twice each year in the US and Europe. We travelled together as a family and had great times. My parents were young enough to enjoy the wonder of the different states in America and we were popular, not just with the press and public, but also with the young ladies.

I found to my pleasant surprise that my darker skin was definitely an attraction. Young female fans at the tournaments came up to us wanting to be friends, and more than friends. They would come to watch the match, rush after us asking for autographs, shouting our names and clamouring for our attention – a glance, a smile, a word, sometimes an acknowledegement. And after one gave the autograph, a conversation could follow, and perhaps some talk about meeting again – a date. That was simple and always possible. And if it didn't happen at the courts, they followed us to the hotel because when the tournament ended, there was always more play at the hotel.

Each week was a different city or a different country, and I was very happy to have my brothers with me. Sometimes I would travel with my parents to certain events while my brothers played at other events. I have great memories of driving from New York to New Jersey and all across the east coast to play in tournaments where my parents accompanied me and we had the most wonderful experiences. It must be mentioned that in most cities that we visited, Indian families we did not know would call us up and invite us to their homes for dosas, or a great chicken curry, because the Amritraj brothers were in town and they had heard about it on the news.

In 1977, travelling both within the country and back and forth between Europe and India became excessive for all three of us and we decided to finally buy a place together, of course in Los Angeles, and where else but in Marina del Rey, a few minutes from the beach. The Marina, as it was called, was very much a place where singles and young couples lived.

Across the street from us was what you'd now call a multiplex, a cinema with six screens in a lovely little shopping mall. While Vijay and I liked the ladies as much as the next guy, our favourite pastime was to go to the movies as often as possible, and have a coffee and discuss the merits or demerits of the film. Anand preferred, and was rather devoted to, discovering, befriending and entertaining young ladies.

It was the era just after the Beatles and the Rolling Stones had discovered the wonders or, at least, the 'costumes' of India, and the craze had arrived in California with the hippie generation. We were far from being hippies or joining that movement in any way, but when we went to India Anand would buy a large selection of women's kurtas, silver and bead chains, necklaces, bracelets and bangles and sandals. He'd come back to LA with a bag full of this stuff and whenever he had a young lady visiting him he would give her gifts. Vijay and I would come home to our condominium after the movies and there would be his lady friend in the living room, all excited. 'Look what I got, look what I got' was a refrain we got used to.

Tennis was continuing its meteoric rise in the late 1970s, and most newspapers and magazines were writing about the ABC of tennis: Amritraj, Borg, Connors. It was a great era for the game, with colourful players, very different from how it is today. Nastase, Borg, Gerulaitis, McEnroe, Vilas were all interesting and entertaining both on and off the court. We were just transitioning from the wood tennis rackets to the metal rackets, which Connors had started playing with and gave more power to the game.

1978 was a truly magical year for me. I once again played in a number of individual tournaments around the country, and then in the summer we gathered in Los Angeles to play those eight weeks of World Team Tennis. Vijay and I were playing for LA along with Ilie Nastase, who was our captain/coach and Chris Evert, who was one of the three female players on our team. Anand was playing for San Diego, just two hours south of us, and most of the top tennis players, male and female, of that era were part of one team or another. Martina Navratilova played for Boston, Billie Jean King for San Francisco, Borg, Gerulaitis and others for various other teams. It was the strongest and most successful year of WTT. The television coverage had grown, and so had the sponsorship and the number of people coming to the Forum to watch the matches. We had packed stands and cheerleaders, not unlike a football or basketball match.

Many nights, after we finished our home matches, Jerry Buss, who owned the team, would say, 'Go and invite anyone from the audience for dinner.' So we would pick the girls who caught our fancy and invite them to dinner that evening. There would be a crowd of Jerry's guests, their friends and ours, perhaps twenty-five people in all, and we would travel in half-a-dozen limos to dinner.

When we finished dinner, Jerry didn't appear to be paying the bill for it. He and his guests, the lot of us would just walk away. I was intrigued and after four or five times I asked Jerry who was paying for these dinners. 'Ashok, try to understand. I give them seats at the Forum and they give me and my friends dinner in their nice restaurants, and provide me limos – barter, a very important lesson.' Jerry was a consummate businessman. At the time I looked upon him as one of the older guys, a sort of godfather figure, but now I realize he must have been only in his early forties.

I played doubles with Vijay through that whole season, and having made it to the playoffs, Jerry Buss was incredibly keen and focused on us winning the playoffs and the championship. Vijay and I remained unbeaten in our doubles matches throughout the playoffs. Vijay and Nastase used to alternate playing the singles. We played Boston in the finals, and ended up winning an extremely close and difficult match. I have, in my home and in my office, the framed photograph of the winning team from 1978 – a memorable moment in my tennis career. Jerry was ecstatic and the following day, having named me the 'most valuable player' in the team, invited me to his office.

I remember walking into his office and him saying, 'I want to thank you. It could not have been done without you.' Then he handed me a key on a keychain. 'Look out of the window,' he said, 'that's your bonus.'

'I thought we already got our bonus,' I said as I looked out of the window. There stood a burgundy Jaguar. It was unbelievable.

That was a highlight of my tennis career – being on the team that won the World Team Tennis championship, and then having the car thrown in!

Jerry went on to buy the Los Angeles Lakers, and became an iconic figure in US sports. It was a great loss to sports fans everywhere and to me personally when he recently passed away.

Another great moment that comes to mind was playing doubles with the legendary Ken Rosewall, the Australian champion. It happened by chance. We were scheduled to play in St. Louis, Missouri, and each of our doubles partners didn't show up, so we decided to play together. It was great fun and a wonderful learning experience to play with one of the greatest players in the history of the sport.

My parents often came over to the US because all three sons were now there. On one of their visits, my brothers and I took them on a trip to Las Vegas. They were going for the first time and of course they knew that it was a place for gambling and for clubs and pizzazz. My parents were and are not in any way gamblers and they didn't quite go for clubs and pizzazz, but we were going to Vegas as a family.

We stayed at the famous Caesar's Palace. We told our parents that Vegas was very compelling, that it seduced you into leaving your money behind. My dad said, 'Don't worry, we don't gamble.' Oh yeah? Well, for the next two days all they did was gamble. They emerged from the casino on the third day looking rather self-conscious, even worried.

We said, 'It's okay, how much money did you lose?', and my dad said that mom had won 200 bucks and he had won 300.

So naturally we asked why they were looking unhappy about it.

They looked at each other. 'Well, if everybody wins this kind of money,' my dad said, 'the place will close down. And we don't want it to. We had such a great time!'

My parents came to visit us often in Marina del Rey, and while Vijay and Anand were on the road playing tournaments, I enjoyed spending time with them. We would, I remember, go quite often to the restaurants on Admiralty Way. They were right on the beach. The Chart House comes to mind. We would sit on the patio and watch the boats during happy hour, when the drinks were served for free. This is where I started developing my taste for wine. My parents and I would have a glass, and it was a magical time as the sun went down and we would talk about India and Europe, the trips we had taken, and the trips we were going to take as a family. These were unforgettable times with my parents that I deeply cherish, and have been uppermost in my mind as I write this book. Wine has since become a great passion of mine, and today a vineyard in Malibu has created a superb limited edition Cabernet red wine and Chardonnay white wine under the Ashok Amritraj label. Who knew, all those years ago when we were at the Chart House getting free drinks during happy hour, that I would have my own wine label?

Sometime in 1980 Anand announced that he was getting married. He was proposing to marry a non-Indian girl. To put it mildly, there was a lot of resistance (the shit hit the fan) from my parents who thought of Anand as our Prince of Wales.

But Anand and Helen were in love and love doesn't always recognize boundaries of race, caste, religion etc. She was an American from an Italian background, both her parents being first generation Italian-Americans. They lived in New York. She was startlingly blonde and beautiful in the mode of Farrah Fawcett, one of the original Charlie's Angels.

Anand and Helen stayed firm in their decision and we brothers sort of fell in with what was to us a progressive concept and so finally my parents agreed. Helen was born a Roman Catholic and the church, unlike us, never made racial distinctions. They were married in a beautiful ceremony at St. Patrick's Cathedral in New York, followed by a reception given by Helen's parents, and another in India by my parents.

Helen is one of four sisters. The family is devout Catholic and very close, much like our own family and that closeness was apparent and appreciated as it made Helen very much of a family person, almost South Indian, as one of my outspoken aunts might have said. Some thirty years later, she is certainly a cherished part of our family.

The idea of being single and carefree and being a part of such a close family is something one does not fully appreciate when one is going through it, but looking back I must admit that if I could relive any portion of my life, it would probably be those years when we were all together, and life was wonderful in its simplicity. As far as the three of us went, we were all single, and as a trio, we felt we were invincible.

When Anand got married in October of 1980, that era of our life was over. As it happened, Vijay and I formed Amritraj Productions that same month.

ATTENBOROUGH, SINATRA AND THE OSCAR

I CONTINUED TO PLAY professional tennis with my brothers all through the 1970s until late 1980. In India, we were the first family of tennis – in fact, the first family of sports – and were iconic figures. This made the decision of giving up tennis, where we had movie star status, and switching, in the late months of 1980, to an industry I knew nothing about but had only dreamt of, much more difficult.

Fifteen months after Anand got married, Vijay got married and we moved from the Marina del Rey house to Sherman Oaks. I shared the house now with Vijay and his wife Shyamala. Playing tennis with the stars and producers and hearing them talk about their deals and the movies was quite tantalizing, but their world seemed closed. There was some mysterious quantum leap between being out of it and being in it – especially for me, as no Indian had ever penetrated this great factory of myth and dream. Not having the 'open sesame' mantra that would start the rock rumbling and pull it aside so I could enter the cave of treasure, I decided to do the next best thing: bang so hard on it that I could not be ignored.

I desperately wanted to learn about the film business and had spent a significant amount of time hanging around edit rooms in the evenings and into the night and visiting film and television sets where my friends would be shooting. Sidney Poitier, one of my early friends in Hollywood, was directing some movies at the time and would let me watch him edit, taking me through the logic of putting a sequence and a story together.

I was trying to pick up as much as I could before taking what I thought would be the big step. But this process of learning new tricks intruded on the perfection of the old. Tennis at the level we played it requires 110 per cent concentration and dedication as does, I soon discovered, the entertainment business. My tennis began to suffer the erosion and pay the price.

My brothers picked up on this fact first and it led to long and heart-searching conversations. I spoke to my parents about the crucial decision – not to give up tennis at all, but to let it take second place to trying to enter the movie business.

Needless to say, my parents were not enthusiastic about the decision. Quite the opposite. Their attitude was simple. What had our family got to do with the movie business? Apart from the fact that my father had once, after performing in a college play, been offered a role and perhaps a career by one of South India's leading movie producers, we had no connection with film or stage or anything of the sort. I had worked my whole life towards a career in tennis. Why would I give it up at this stage of the game? To quit while I was being told I had so much promise? I had many long discussions with Vijay, who was very keen on being an actor, but his tennis career was going so well he did not have enough time for it. (Though he did do a memorable acting turn in the James Bond film *Octopussy*.)

I considered taking the plunge. The challenge, the possibility, the decision to break away from what I knew, and from what I had a future in, and enter the unknown was with me night and day. It wasn't a challenge anyone else had posed to me. It was something I was daring myself to do. Suppose I jumped, where would I land? Where would the challenge lead? It was daunting. I can't pinpoint the exact moment I took the decision to throw caution to the winds and take the leap. It was a direction in which I felt compelled to go, to grasp a possible future. It was in the 'possible' that the dilemma lay. If I have one bit of advice for the next generation, I would say, follow your passion, understand when you need to change direction, and then have the guts to follow through and do it.

Now, years later, I can recall the poem by Robert Frost which so beautifully encapsulates the questions of human choice. It's called 'The Road Not Taken', and is worth quoting:

I shall be telling this with a sigh
Somewhere ages and ages hence:
two roads diverged in a wood, and I,
I took the one less travelled by,
And that has made all the difference

In late 1980, after one of the various conversations Vijay and I had, Vijay talked to Al Hill Jr about a movie partnership, and Al sent his private plane to fly me to Dallas. Al was the nephew of Lamar Hunt of the legendary Hunt family and both sponsored and owned the World Championship Tennis tour, a professional tour. Al was very close to Vijay and had often said to him that he wanted to enter the entertainment and movie business. The meeting went very well and the three of us decided we would start a movie company together. We would develop movies and once fully developed, find the funding for them and Al would provide the overhead. So, late in

1980 we formed Amritraj Productions with Al, Vijay and myself as partners. We chose the name not out of vanity but out of the hope that our prominence in the tennis field, the amount of coverage we had received for it and the network we had built as the Amritraj brothers would give us a recognition factor in Hollywood.

Al Hill lived and worked in Dallas. Vijay was still playing professional tennis and was in and out of the office and the new business. I was left running the company.

I spent the next four years trying to really learn the trade. The fascination for films had to now translate into the nitty-gritty and mechanics of creating coherent visions from scratch. One of the people who befriended me at that time was Sid Balkin. He had worked in the industry for many years and he came on board as a consultant to the company. It was he who gave me my first basic education about scripts – how to read them, how to project the word on the page imaginatively onto the possibilities on screen, how to identify the flaws and gaps in vision and even how to gently interpose one's script editing without offending the creative sensibilities, or indeed the ego, of the writers.

Sid had worked for a long time with Bill Castle, a well-known figure in the challenging low-budget world of Hollywood. Castle was born William Schloss, but translated his surname (which means 'castle' in German) in order to get on in Hollywood. He was something of a legend. He had worked on Broadway in his youth and had been an assistant director to Orson Welles. When he began to produce and direct his own films, he became famous for his promotional gimmicks.

Sid told me a story about the film *Macabre* which Castle made and released in 1958. Castle emphasized the thriller element of his film by handing out to the audience $1,000 life insurance policies from Lloyd's of London in case they should die of fright during the film. Showings also had nurses stationed in the lobbies and hearses parked outside the theatre. For the exhibition of a film called *Tingler*, Castle fitted the audience seats with mild electric shocks and for another film he invented what he called the Coward's Corner, a cardboard booth into which anyone who couldn't withstand the horror the movie supposedly created could walk into in front of the rest of the audience.

The bizarre stories demonstrated that in Hollywood, if one had the streak of inventiveness, one could survive by one's wits. Sid also said that after making sixty-three films, Bill Castle went from eccentric to literally crazy. This is not an uncommon story of the pressure that comes with success.

It was an early lesson on the importance of marketing and distribution of films. 50 per cent of film-making is developing the screenplay and producing the film, and the other 50 per cent is making sure people are aware of your movie and want to see it. With the remarkable number of electronic devices, social networking and various forms of home entertainment available today, this lesson is more important than ever before.

Amritraj Productions began by developing a couple of projects, one called *Damn Yankees* (based on the Broadway play) and the other called *Nine Tiger Man*, a tale set in India during the Raj. The prospects were not bright. I had no idea how to develop a good script or how to raise money for production. I still remember that period as the dark days. I was learning various lessons on how to get a picture made.

Yes, we had called our firm Amritraj Productions, relying on our tennis connections to provide a smooth opening. I began to see that my proficiency at tennis was a double-edged sword, a poisoned chalice, or whatever metaphor tells you that on the one hand it helped me make connections, but on the other pigeonholed me as a tennis player and prevented me from being taken seriously as a movie maker.

Tennis was certainly an easy way of being introduced on intimate terms to celebrities and studio executives, and I was under the illusion that the introductions would lead me into the profession of movies.

I was naïve to think it. The executives and moghuls who played with me naturally thought of me as the tennis player, and not 'a player'. An example of this was when I sent a script over to a studio head whose house I also played tennis at. A couple of weeks later I called him up and he spent about fifteen minutes on the phone with me. Now this would sound very promising except for the fact that over fourteen-and-a-half of the fifteen minutes were about his backhand and his second serve, and the advice he needed to make it better. As the call was winding down, I quickly asked, 'What did you think of the script I gave you?'

'The script? What ... oh the script? Yeah, no we passed on that weeks ago.'

What matters is not what life throws at you, it's how you respond to it. Tennis got my foot in the door, but would it prise that door of a very protected and seemingly self-sufficient mansion open?

There was another factor that was inhibiting, and a challenge. No Indian had ever broken into Fortress Hollywood and India, unlike today, was a land far, far away. 'Bollywood' was not in the Western vocabulary; it was an unknown word.

Americans have always manifested a certain uncertainty about world geography. It comes of course from the conceit that the US of A is the centre of the universe, much as the medieval Chinese believed that their country was middle earth. One of the stories about President Ronald Reagan was that in 1983 he was told that there was a danger that a communist government would establish itself in Grenada and make an alliance with Cuba. There was fighting inside the ruling party and his advisors felt that the US should send in the marines. Reagan said yes, he agreed, the marines should go in and restore order and stop the communist riots and 'where the hell is Grenada?'

The stereotype was confirmed for me when in a conversation with a studio boss, who could boast a modest American school and college education, I was asked where I came from and when I said India, he responded, 'Oh yes, of course! I've always loved Singapore. By the way, which part of India is Singapore in?'

Sidney Poitier had now become a close friend and his story of the struggle to be at first a black actor and then a director in the industry was inspiring and heartbreaking at the same time. Yes, the African-American race had fought for a deserved place in the dreamscape of Hollywood because that race had been part of America through painful, horrific beginnings to claiming their place. We subcontinental Indians had arrived of late. We were just about beginning to find a foothold in America. For me, with my ambition of entering Hollywood, there was no path chalked out and no role models. Here I was, like the Greeks outside Troy, camped on the sands with this impregnable fortress before me. What equivalent of a Trojan horse could I build for the insiders to open the gates?

If I remember right, this period of relegation, of hanging about, of knocking on doors till my knuckles had turned from brown to red to grey, lasted five long years. Vijay and Anand meanwhile continued to play tennis, doing extremely well, not being under the pressures and disappointments of my ambition. I would watch their matches on TV and wonder if I had made a huge mistake. I must also say that it was a lonely time switching careers. I was making a little headway but I wasn't making either money or films.

It was in this state of semi-despair that I first met Richard Attenborough. My dear friend Jake Eberts (who recently passed away and whose wife years later would photograph my wedding for the UK *Daily Telegraph*) was running a company called Goldcrest, based in London, and had made waves with *Chariots of Fire*, directed by Hugh Hudson. It won several Oscars and now his company was engaged in the making of the epic *Gandhi*. They were shooting in India.

Jake, a huge tennis fan, and I were developing *Nine Tiger Man* together. He proposed that we go to India. It was a very welcome proposition for three reasons. We could look around the Raj settings that were to be a part of *Nine Tiger Man*, I could get back to a country I was familiar with, and yes, we would see *Gandhi* being filmed. At that time it was arousing the curiosity of Hollywood and the world – with its Indian icon, a man of the century and with its historical background. I felt somewhat possessive about the prospect if not about the project.

Jake and I spent a day on the sets of *Gandhi*. Richard Attenborough couldn't have been nicer. He was extremely proud of what he was doing and was facing the trials and tribulations of shooting in India, and putting together something that hadn't been attempted before with the greatest of patience and good humour.

He had the knack or gift of making you feel special in his presence, as though all his concentration was on you, even though you knew that there were a million considerations he had to keep his eye on. Or at least the corner of his eye!

Some thirty years later, Dickie (Richard) would come to my hotel to 'pitch me a project'. He was frail and in a wheelchair, having recently recovered from a stroke. We spent an hour talking about how inspired I was on the sets of *Gandhi*. Unfortunately, the project Dickie presented was not one I responded to, and I felt quite broken up by the fact that there was no way I could help this extraordinary director who had provided such inspiration to my career.

There were happier ripples of my trip to India. I got to know the star who played Gandhi, now Sir Ben Kingsley, and hosted a dinner party for him when he received his star on the Hollywood Walk of Fame.

I returned to LA and the following year, after the worldwide release of *Gandhi*, was invited by a friend, who worked for *The Hollywood Reporter* magazine, to attend the Oscars. It was 1982, my first time.

Los Angeles stops on Oscar day. The roads and freeways are clogged with the limos and cars carrying the stars, the guests and the onlookers bumper to bumper in what they call a 'gridlock'. One starts out for the venue hours before time. One gets to the entrance of the venue, the Dorothy Chandler Pavilion (or today, the Dolby Theatre), and alights with the carpet laid out and the police keeping the applauding throngs back. The fans, an orderly mob usually, shout and scream the names of their favourite stars as they step out of their limos, appealing to them for a glance or a wave.

Inside the auditorium the cameras record the ceremony on stage as well as the celebrities in the audience. Out of view, lining the walls, are the 'extras', men in tuxedos and frock coats. They line the walls out of sight of the cameras, waiting throughout the long ceremony for any of the guests to go to the washroom. The stewards then immediately substitute one of these extras in the vacant seat. The hall must look absolutely packed for the cameras at all times. A small but indicative Hollywood illusion – no one goes to the washroom!

That year *Gandhi* won Best Film and several other accolades. Attenborough gave his famous acceptance speech in which he paid tribute to the Mahatma and his dedication to historical change without violence. I felt part of it, as a friend of the *Gandhi* team and, most of all, as a proud Indian.

In the early 1980s, I was working hard at learning my craft as a movie producer, and at the same time a part of me felt that I really wanted to respect my years of tennis. Memorable evenings were spent with Tom Laughlin who was a big deal in the movie business at the time. He had done *Billie Jack*, a very popular film that he produced and starred in. Saturday afternoon games at his home in Brentwood included movie stars like Clint Eastwood, Gene Wilder, Farrah Fawcett, Mel Brooks, Sidney Poitier and Carl Reiner. We'd meet, play tennis in the afternoon, jump in the pool, relax in the jacuzzi and watch movies as it got dark. A big screen would drop from the ceiling and we would see private viewings of movies that hadn't yet been released.

What did that do for a young man from Chennai with dreams? Watching a screening with Sidney Poitier, Gene Wilder and others was, to say the least, pretty amazing. Those afternoons must have made a significant impact on me, since for the last decade or more I have similar games at my home on Saturday mornings with stars and studio executives.

The circle of friends that I made through tennis soon became wider and invitations to play tennis with stars and executives came from all over the world. I was called to various celebrity and charity events which was not only delightful, but also taught me about philanthropy, giving back to those less fortunate and raising money for various causes. This was a valuable lesson, and over the last two decades, philanthropy has been an important part of my life.

One such charity event was at Monte Carlo, hosted by Prince Rainier and his son Prince Albert (the current ruler of Monaco) to benefit the Princess Grace Foundation for the Arts. In 1987, at the event, I found myself in the company of Princess Stephanie and we became good friends.

One night, she invited me to join her and a few friends at a popular night club in Monaco which she frequented.

It was a great evening and having released her security for the night, I was driving her back in the wee hours of the morning along the curvy coastal road of the principality of Monaco that runs parallel to the Mediterranean, perhaps the very road where her mother Princess Grace was killed in a car accident. We were chatting away and I didn't notice the speed I was driving at till the blue lights of the police squad car and its siren behind me drew my attention to the fact that I was exceeding the limit. The car and a motorcycle came up behind me even as I slowed down on the road that wound up to the cliffs of Monaco. The motorcycle policeman waved me down, motioning me to stop.

'Damn, I'm sorry. Got absorbed, didn't notice the speed,' I muttered to the princess as we came to a halt and the Monegasque police squad car drew up behind me.

I was about to get out of my car when Stephanie said, 'Don't worry, stay inside.' She pushed the button to wind the window down. I did the same.

The police officers came to my side. The princess turned the internal cab light on and in a very polite tone said, 'Good evening, officers. Lovely evening, isn't it?'

They instantly recognized her, took two steps back, saluted smartly and said, 'Yes, Your Highness.' Then, 'Please proceed, sir,' one of them mumbled, not wanting to detain me a second longer.

We drove away. 'They may tail us just to see that we are all right,' she said, 'so don't worry if they follow.'

It must be nice to own a country!

On another occasion, I played doubles at the Monaco event with Barbara Sinatra (yes, Frank's wife), and every night Frank would take a group of us out to dinner. It was an extraordinary experience, because if there was royalty of Hollywood at the time, Frank was certainly the high-ranking monarch. He was the Chairman of the Board (a title used to describe Sinatra during his decades as an icon). And here I was, a small-movie maker, having dinner and chatting with him!

After the first three or four nights, I suppose through Frank's choice, the company boiled down to Frank and Barbara, Roger Moore and his wife at the time, Luisa, Bernie Kopell who was doing a series called *The Love Boat* then, and myself. There were two other people who were indispensable. One was Gilly Mack, Frank's bodyguard, and the other was his personal priest, Father Blewitt, from Newport Beach. They were inseparable and I figured that Frank required one for the well-being of his body and the other for the well-being of his soul, which was fair enough.

The last evening we, the Sinatra entourage, were at dinner at the Hotel de Paris and I wanted to go, as I did each year, to try my luck at the fabled tables at the Casino De Paris. I was sitting next to Roger at dinner and after the last course I whispered to him, 'I'm going to slide out and the party's going so well, I don't think Frank will mind or even notice.'

'You can't leave before the chairman,' Roger said.

'I really don't think he'll notice,' I said.

I was wrong. He noticed. As I rose to vanish as inconspicuously as I could, he shouted across, 'Ashok, where are you going?'

I shrugged. 'Well, I have this sort of tradition: every time I come to Monaco, I lose a few hundred dollars at the Casino de Paris and seeing as it's our last night, I thought I'd keep up that tradition and make my donation to those who have too much anyway.'

'That sounds like a great tradition and fun. Roger and I will join you.'

That was a welcome surprise and so Roger, Frank and I walked over in the moonlight to the Casino de Paris.

Frank said he was not a gambling man, not that night anyway.

The casino is a magnificent building off a paved square and it's built like a palace. Frank and Roger said they'd sit in the vast lobby and smoke their post-prandial cigars while I went in and played. That was fine with me. I sauntered in, played a little blackjack, and then went on to the table to shoot craps (play dice). An hour passed and I had lost about $400 and decided to call it a day. I emerged from the gaming room and Frank asked me how I'd done, how Lady Luck had treated me. People looked on incredulously, shaking their heads as though to confirm to themselves that they must be mistaken, that it couldn't be Frank Sinatra and Roger Moore sitting there smoking cigars. Those had to be people who resembled them.

'So? How much did you lose?' Roger asked.

'Four hundred dollars,' I said. And just as we were stepping out of the casino the manager came running up behind us. He handed me an envelope. We stopped and I looked inside. Four hundred dollars.

'What's this?' I asked the manager.

'When you come to our casino with Mr Sinatra,' he said, 'you don't lose.'

'And what would have happened if I'd won?'

'Oh, we are always happy when our customers win,' he said, grinning.

Can one forget such an evening?

THE SCHOOL OF HARD KNOCKS

I WAS NOT GETTING many incoming calls, but I would put all the lines on my office phone on hold so that to those people calling in I would appear to be incredibly busy, as they could not get through.

Meanwhile, I was, in order to pick up experience and in furtherance of our company, reading scripts diligently. It occurred to me that reading scripts was the natural way to start. There were some I really liked and thought I saw potential in but I must admit now that I had not the faintest idea how to get a movie made. One read a script and felt that if it was good it should get made. But that's not the way Hollywood works!

In 1981, needing help from an experienced producer, I brought *Damn Yankees* to the attention of Bernard Schwartz who had previously made *Coal Miner's Daughter*, and together we took it to Universal Studios. After a two-year development period at the studio, we were finally gearing up to make it. The head of production at Universal at the time was Ned Tannen who was about to 'green light' the film when he stepped down from his position and was replaced by Frank Price.

We then heard that Frank was putting our movie in 'turnaround' which means the studio would not finance its production and we could buy the script back when we wanted it or had prospects elsewhere. I was learning. Not only the ways of the studios but their jargon: the 'green light', 'turnaround', 'pay or play', 'waterfall' ...

When the personnel of studios or, for that matter independent film or TV companies, change, they bring their own tastes and criteria with them and are in very many instances, if not always, contemptuous of the decisions and artistic and commercial acumen and choices of their predecessors. It's almost always 'all change'. And Frank Price put about sixty projects into turnaround at Universal when he took over. I suppose it must be the same in other businesses – the new manager of the hotel changes the menu and the décor, the new curator of the Louvre takes down and dumps all the old paintings, the Rembrandts and Da Vincis ... er ... perhaps not! Maybe the entertainment industry is unique in this respect.

So *Damn Yankees* was back with us but what were we to do with it? A similar fate awaited *Nine Tiger Man* which I had developed at Goldcrest with my friend Jake Eberts. We took it to 20th Century Fox where Sherry Lansing was president. The studio paid for a rewrite of the screenplay. The man who had brought us the screenplay in the first place was a producer called Michael Deeley who had won an Oscar for *The Deerhunter*. With his credentials we thought we were very close to getting the movie made. It never happened. The money men (or women in this case) didn't see the potential for success that we saw and the script languishes to this day. Incidentally, I hear on the grapevine that a studio is today, thirty years later, trying to remake *Damn Yankees*.

Film is unlike any other art because it is part business, part gamble, part bravado. To write a poem costs the poet his or her emotional and intellectual engagement and a certain amount of time, but it is an individual creation. So also with painting and writing novels and still photography. Cinema is quintessentially the art form of the developed capitalist era. Yes, it takes art and creativity in huge doses, but it costs money and those who are putting in the money want returns. Like any businessmen they make a calculation on the returns and soon a formula evolves. Get the hottest stars, find the theme that the ethos of the age is obsessed with, build drama, suspense and create a spectacle through the tried and tested methods ... yes, yes yes, but we end up with a formula.

One of the wisest and boldest things the great novelist and screenplay writer William Goldman said in his seminal book *Adventures in the Screen Trade* about the Hollywood experience was, 'No one knows anything!'

I would add to that. Studio heads and others who determine the investment of hundreds of millions in movies are appointed because they think, or others think, they know something. They have the formula or some talent which takes them beyond the formula.

The truth is that Hollywood is like gambling on the horses. There are favourites and jockeys who have performed brilliantly, there are known conditions on race courses. There are short odds on favourites and long odds on the outsiders, and the millions spent on publicizing a film and persuading the world that they must see it is somewhat equivalent to fixing a race.

And then William Goldman's truth comes into play. No one knows anything! The outsider on long odds wins, the favourite flounders, the formula has to be reassessed. Oh fickle public! Oh quagmire of an industry! But did I then, and now, still want to be a part of it?

You bet.

There was one maxim I had to follow: Don't relax. This is a race, not a hundred-metre dash but a marathon, and it may not be one against others but one against yourself. Which brings to mind a poem I vaguely remember from school. It's one of the most famous poems in the English language and I couldn't recite all of it, but I remember its theme and looked up *If*.

It is in the main a prescription for a generous and active code of behaviour, a message of nobility. Yet its premise is that to 'be a man', as Rudyard Kipling puts it, meaning to be a complete and good human being, one has to make the right choices. The poem is not a meditation on luck and chance but reading it one can see that the road prescribed by Kipling is hard and exacting and one could easily slip into the opposite direction:

> *If you can keep your head when all about you*
> *Are losing theirs and blaming it on you ...*
> *If you can dream – and not make dreams your master;*
> *If you can think – and not make thoughts your aim;*
> *If you can meet with Triumph and Disaster*
> *And treat those two impostors just the same ...*
> *If you can talk with crowds and keep your virtue,*
> *Or walk with Kings – nor lose the common touch ...*
>
> *If you can fill the unforgiving minute*
> *With sixty seconds' worth of distance run,*
> *Yours is the Earth and everything that's in it,*
> *And – which is more – you'll be a Man, my son!*

By the end of four years, the development deals had not amounted to much. Both *Nine Tiger Man* and *Damn Yankees* were in turnaround, not moving ahead. Finally, in 1984, Vijay and I raised a little money from some Indian friends, half a million dollars to be exact, and I produced a film called *Fear in a Handful of Dust*. It was based on a novel by Brian Garfield. Brian had come to fame by writing *Death Wish*, the Charles Bronson movie.

The title of his novel, and of the movie we were about to make, was taken from T.S. Eliot's poem 'The Waste Land'. If I remember right, the line is: 'I will show you fear in a handful of dust.' And the theme of the script justified the quote. It was a story to be shot in an arid landscape. We found the locations in the Arizona desert and we were scheduled there for a four-week shoot. The set in the desert didn't offer much variation, so the pictorial background, while remaining key to the story and its symbolism, was not varied.

This gave the filming the quality of shooting a stage play where the acting mattered most. I loved every bit of it – the work, watching the drama take shape and, surprisingly, being out there in the desert. It was my first experience of working with actors, which was fascinating. Three out of the four were really professional, with the fourth turning out to be – how shall I put it? – more than a little problematic. We didn't know it when we cast him, but he was a lover of the 'bottle' and didn't confine his tastes to the twilight hours.

He would wander off to the town and on one of these wanderings was arrested for being drunk and disorderly. We had to get him out of jail pronto as every minute on a set, on a film shoot, costs the salaries of everyone else and the hire of the equipment and much more besides. Most importantly, on a $500,000 budget I could not afford to have one of my actors in jail.

Besides getting thrown in jail and being hauled out, he behaved disgracefully at the end of the shoot, at the wrap party to which we had invited important guests. He was as usual inebriated and exposed himself, peed in public and had to be restrained and seen off.

That was, in terms of what can happen on film shoots, a small hiccup and for me it was an interesting first experience of making a movie. It worked nevertheless and was distributed successfully by Hemdale, known later for distributing hit films such as *The Terminator* and *Platoon*.

It was that same year, 1984, that I had my first encounter with Jean Claude Van Damme. I was sitting in my office one day, hoping to get *Fear in a Handful of Dust* off the ground. I opened my mail with my fingers crossed: there would be a bite on one of my projects, backing for a script I'd sent around, Stallone or Steve Martin would have written saying they were dying to work with me ... well it wasn't any of these but inside a manila envelope were 8x10' photographs of a young man, posing in the usual way, trying to look charming, menacing, boy-next-door, glamour model in turns. A picture which caught my attention was one where his legs were spread in a completely horizontal split. Attached was a letter. The writer, the person in the photographs, said he wanted to act in Hollywood movies.

I knew that producers received such letters of self-introduction as a matter of ever overwhelming routine, but at the time and the stage of the game at which I was in, I didn't get too many of them. The letter, which wasn't entirely grammatical, intrigued me. It gave me a phone number which I called.

The rest, as recalled in an earlier chapter, including my second encounter with Jean Claude six years later at the Cannes Film Festival, led to us working together on *Double Impact*, a film that affected both our fortunes.

In 1985 I met the legendary Roger Corman and when I say

'legendary' I don't say it carelessly. He was and is still a legend in Hollywood. His autobiography is titled *How I Made a Hundred Movies in Hollywood and Never Lost a Dime*. And it's no lie. In fact Roger as writer, director, producer or executive producer made more than 350 movies and never lost that particular dime (he kept it carefully in his pocket). He was the king of the low-budget movie and he originated a modus operandi which ensured that the cost of the product would be covered by commitments for its sale. In most cases his films were pre-sold. It sounds like common sense and elementary logic, but Hollywood costs and sales are not arithmetic; they are more of a complex algebra, with a touch of wizardry. I learned the former from Roger.

Roger also has the distinction of starting many Hollywood superstars in their careers. Francis Copolla, Jack Nicholson and Ron Howard are amongst those who worked with him or for him early in their careers. Discovering new talent was also a lesson learned from Roger, and over my career I have had the good fortune of discovering some talented actors, directors and writers.

At the time I met Roger, the market for films on VHS and the format called Betamax was opening up and reaching its peak. There was no DVD format yet. Technology has progressively created other opportunities and will no doubt continue to do so faster over the next decade than in any other era. There are young film-makers today creating content straight for the web – YouTube for example, which was not even a thought in the 1980s.

The new technology of the time, though outdated now, was an opportunity that Roger spotted. People wouldn't go to the theatre, they'd rent or buy a movie from a store on VHS and as far as the film-makers were concerned, there'd be an after-life for the product on television. I too saw the opportunity and took it, together with Roger. We made about half-a-dozen movies together.

It proved to be a huge marketplace. A number of new companies got into it: there was HBO, Showtime and USA Networks and they started making movies – movies of the week and other strategies to gain viewership and branding. It was fertile ground to cut my teeth on.

For the next five years, I ignored the studio world and got very deeply into the world of independent film-making. The budgets, using these new techniques and formats, were initially from half-a-million dollars to one and half million. As I got more successful, I made movies for two million and then five million dollars. The education received from these movies was irreplaceable and the one constant was that there is no replacement for good, old-fashioned hard work, and that I did! Twenty-four hours a day, seven days a week.

1985. I made an action film called *Nine Deaths of the Ninja*. During the shoot my lead actor started an affair with a girl who happened to be the girlfriend of the head of the Yakuza, which is the underground Japanese Triad organization, the powerful and threatening far-eastern mafia. This Capo di Capi came to me and threatened to kill all of us unless my lead actor stopped his affair with his mistress. Every human being knows or should know that it's impossible to argue with someone in love. There was nothing I or anyone could say to our lead actor. Desperate remedies were called for. I phoned the actor's wife and family in the US and offered them a free holiday during the shoot. I didn't of course tell the wife why, but flew her in and alerted her husband about the great news: his wife and children were arriving from LA to support him. He came to his senses and the affair stopped. This is

My mother Maggie Amritraj, 1953.   My father Robert Amritraj, 1953.

Oldest to youngest: brothers Anand (six), Vijay (four) and me (one), 1957.

Aged thirteen, flanked by my brothers in Madras, 1969.

The Amritraj brothers outside the Gloucester Hotel, London, 1974.

Winning the World Team Tennis Championships at the Fabulous Forum in 1978. Jerry Buss (owner), Bill Norris (trainer), me, Ann Kiyomura, Illie Nastase, Chris Evert, Stephanie Tolleson and Vijay Amritraj.

Greeting Prime Minister Rajiv Gandhi with my parents and brothers, 1987.

On the pro tour, late 1970s.

With Sir Sean Connery, 1990.

A tennis game with His Serene
Highness Prince Albert II
of Monaco, 1986.

Clowning around with Sir Roger
Moore, Mike Douglas and Harry
Belafonte in Monaco, 1987.

Chitra and me at our wedding,
5 September 1991.

With President Ronald Reagan and First Lady Nancy Reagan at
the White House, 1992.

Priya's first holy communion, 2002.

The Amritraj family on holiday in India, 2012.

After a couple of glasses of wine, the three Amritraj brothers in 2009.

With Sidney Poitier
at a friend's house
for dinner, 1988.

On the Lantau Island
location of *Double
Impact*, with ICM
agent Jack Gilardi,
Jean Claude Van
Damme and Geoffrey
Lewis, 1990.

Partying with
M. Night Shyamalan and
Dustin Hoffman, 2002.

Filming *Bringing
Down the House*
with Steve Martin,
2002.

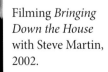

Variety magazine's celebration of my hundreth film, with *Variety's* Steven Gaydos (executive editor) and Tim Grey (editor in chief), 2010.

Randall Wallace (the Oscar-nominated screenwriter of *Braveheart*), Shah Rukh Khan and Victoria Pearman (Mick Jagger's production partner) at my party for *Paheli*, 2006.

World premiere of *Dreamer* with Goldie Hawn and Kurt Russell, 2005.

With Sir Ben Kingsley at my party for his star on the Hollywood Walk of Fame, 2011.

Receiving my induction plaque into the Academy of Motion Pictures Arts and Sciences from Charlton Heston, 1992.

At the premiere of *Shopgirl* with Claire Danes, 2005.

Moonlight Mile premiere with Jake Gyllenhaal, 2002.

Raising Helen world premiere at the opening night of the Tribeca Film Festival in NYC—with Robert De Niro, Kate Hudson, Garry Marshall, Hayden Panettiere, John Corbett, Abigail Breslin and Nina Jacobson, 2004.

Trading stories (and punches) with Sly Stallone at the Beverly Hills Hotel, 2008.

Walking Tall premiere with MGM vice-chairman Chris McGurk and Dwayne 'The Rock' Johnson, 2004.

On the set of *Bandits* with Cate Blanchett, 2000.

Moonlight Mile premiere with Dustin Hoffman, 2002.

With MGM vice-chairman Chris McGurk and Michael Douglas, 2004.

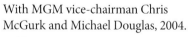

With Shankar,
Aishwarya Rai,
Subhash Ghai and
Prashanth at the
rainy muhurtham
of *Jeans*, 1996.

Rajnikanth arrives
with an entourage
of reporters.

Kamal Hassan arrives.

Being interviewed
by Karan Johar at
FICCI Frames, 2006.

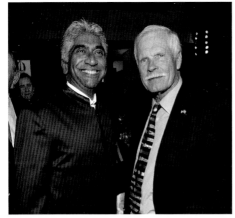

With CNN's Ted Turner at the United Nations' dinner for 'Every Woman, Every Child', 2012.

With Mohamed Al Mubarak (chairman of Image Nation), and Michael Garin (CEO of Image Nation), Abu Dhabi, 2012.

On the set of *Ghost Rider: Spirit of Vengeance* with Nicolas Cage and the film's directors, Mark Neveldine and Brian Taylor, 2011.

Thanking the Hollywood community for my Producer of Vision Award, 2004.

Youngest to oldest: me, Vijay and Anand, 1963.

The Amritraj family at our Marina Del Rey home, 1978.

The entire Amritraj family celebrating my parents' sixtieth wedding anniversary, 2009.

one instance of the various strategies that a producer is called upon to deploy, apart from making the film. We call it 'protecting' the actors and the movie.

The movie was distributed by a company called Crown International. It was a success in 1985 in the US and in many parts of the world, but I never saw a cent from the profits. It taught me the power and illusions of bookkeeping in the film industry. Perhaps, more importantly, I learned the hard way that everything depends on the agreement you enter into. I would advise anyone starting in the business to take time out to study the nuances of contracts, the specification of costs and overheads. Often in Hollywood one hears the phrase 'double bookkeeping'. Most times, however, the bookkeeping defines the level of the ladder on which you stand when it comes to returns and how and after whom you get paid.

At the top of the ladder you have a 'gross player', next you may have an 'adjusted gross player', then you have a 'high-end-net-profit player', and then a 'standard net profit player' who gets what's left if there is any left of the 'net'. And between the gross and the net come the accountants. If your contract is not perused by someone who knows the game forwards and backwards, there are never any net profits left to get to those at the bottom of the ladder.

You pay the price for the experience as I did in this case. The price can be millions of dollars. I did not understand the way this stuff worked when I made *Ninja*. The word I learned through these transactions and disappointments was 'waterfall'. It's a metaphor for the flow of revenues from a film. It's like a ladder – the guy at the top of the waterfall gets to drink first. Again the guys on the lower shore better watch out or there'll be no water coming their way. They can see the water falling but they remain thirsty.

The 1980s were the glory days of cinema companies. I wanted

to bring Hollywood to India and India to Hollywood (a trend I continue today) and I had this script called *Bloodstone*, an unusual genre of thriller. One of the most celebrated movie stars of South India, indeed of all India, is Tamil film actor Rajnikanth. In 1984 he wasn't the icon he is today but certainly a star. I wanted to work with him, got in touch and discussed the story with him. Rajni came on board. He was great to work with, the ultimate professional. Besides that he gave superb performances before the camera and supported the rest of the cast with the utmost modesty.

Bloodstone was conceived and shot in English, directed by Dwight Little who went on to make Steven Seagal and Wesley Snipes movies.

The image that stays in my mind is of Rajni, when he was not required on the set, sitting outside it reading a comic book, waiting for his shot rather than retiring to his trailer (or the equivalent in India in those days) or playing the star and demanding attention. He was never late.

By 1987 it became clear that the Amritraj Productions' three-way partnership was not working. Vijay was still busy playing tennis and my other partner, Al Hill, had many other interests and had moved on to several business ventures of his own. What was apparent to me was that running an office and paying the overheads didn't get movies made. Unless an investor was willing to put millions of dollars into making the film in addition to paying the rent for an office, it didn't make sense to have an overhead-paying partner. Not for him and not for me. We discussed it and Al, the first paymaster of Amritraj Productions, decided to move on. Vijay had also come to the conclusion that he would devote his time to his exceptional career in championship tennis.

We dissolved the partnership. I was alone and carried on

knocking on doors, continuing to have the big ones, at the studio level, slammed in my face while I made films with Corman, Hemdale and the indie world, waiting for my break. They say success is when opportunity meets hard work. I was sure I was putting in the hard work. It certainly felt like it. But would opportunity come knocking or is it true that opportunity is only a coming together, a product of a myriad circumstances you have constructed yourself?

Sometime after the dissolution of the partnership, I was presented with the screenplay of a small, interesting thriller called *Snapdragon*. I took it to Prism Entertainment – a company known primarily for distributing video titles in the US – who liked the project, and after some persuasion, agreed to finance it for me.

We cast an extremely popular pin-up, calendar girl type from a successful TV series, in the lead female role. It was her first feature film, so we wanted a young, experienced, talented actor to play the male lead opposite her.

I received a call from an agent at International Creative Management (ICM) – one of the top four talent agencies in the world – who very enthusiastically pitched me the idea of one of his young male clients playing the lead. The actor he suggested had co-starred in a couple of very successful films, and had even been nominated for some major awards. However, I had heard whispers around town that this young man's career was on a downward spiral, as he had become hooked on a variety of illegal substances.

His agent, however, insisted those stories were blown way out of proportion. 'He's completely clean, Ashok,' he assured me. 'I wouldn't represent him otherwise!'

I agreed to meet the actor – we'll call him John – and to my great relief, he seemed an extremely nice, put-together young man. I had enjoyed his past work, and felt he was right for the role, so I called his agent and asked, 'Are you sure John is cleaned up and capable of doing this movie?'

'Absolutely! There is no doubt that John is clean.' (Whatever an agent tells you, always take it with more than a few grains of salt!)

Four days into the shoot, I got a call from the Los Angeles set of the film. It was past noon, and shooting for the day hadn't begun yet. They were hours behind schedule.

I rushed over immediately, found the director, and asked what the problem was.

'John won't come out of his trailer.'

Not good.

I gathered the director and a few crew members, and we approached John's trailer. I banged on the door a few times. No answer. I knocked even louder. Still nothing.

Horrible visions of what we would find behind that door formed in my mind. Clearly, this was now an emergency. We grabbed a screwdriver and jimmied the door open. We found John sitting on the toilet, pants around his ankles, completely passed out. If there was any good news to take away from this situation, it was that he was thankfully still alive. We picked him up off the toilet and splashed water on his face to wake him up.

We called a doctor right away. After examining John, he informed us that he was 'certainly not substance free'. Not knowing anything about drugs, I replied, 'Well, get him off whatever stuff he is on! I need him to work!'

The doctor explained that they would need to combat his addiction with methadone. He would require a little time off, but could get back to work soon.

Naturally, having been assured by ICM that John was

completely clean, I was crazed. The situation had gotten so bad so quickly. I was convinced that John's agent had to have known about his condition all along. I called him saying, 'Did you bullshit me? I just found your client passed out!'

His response: 'That's impossible! He's completely clean!'

I suppose it's possible that John had presented himself to his agents as professionally as he had presented himself to me, and they were able to work closely with him without ever suspecting something was wrong. It's possible, but I didn't believe it for a second.

I had an assistant watch over John day and night, and he came back to work, and dutifully kept up with his methadone doses. He came to me several times on set to say, 'Mr Amritraj, you're saving my life!' Of course, getting off drugs isn't easy, and the shoot still had its share of delays. At one point, during a delicate love scene with the lead actress, John passed out and rested atop her in a very, shall we say, delicate position.

Clearly, they wouldn't teach you about this at any film school. My lower budget movies in those early days taught me more about managing all aspects of a production, interacting with a variety of actors and solving problems on the spur of the moment than I ever could have learned in a classroom.

Waiting for the big break wasn't in itself disconcerting. I told myself I was making headway and there would, with some luck, be a real turning point. I couldn't predict when, though quite often people and press today ask me when I think it was. I don't think one can pinpoint such moments in one's memory. The preparation and the thousand factors that lead to one of those moments are as important as the moment itself.

Today I realize how important the journey I went through and the agonizing years of hard work were. I was lucky I had great teachers. Yes, my first big global success came with Jean Claude and *Double Impact* in 1991, but I certainly didn't become a success overnight.

A little story I heard in Hollywood: Pablo Picasso was drinking his morning coffee at a pavement table of a Paris café when an American lady spotted him and approached him with some trepidation. 'Mr Picasso, my daughter and I are great fans. Would you do me the favour of signing an autograph?'

'Sure,' said Picasso and turning the menu card over to its blank reverse, he sketched the church spire, a woman walking a poodle on the opposite pavement and the general streetscape in front of them. Then he signed it and handed the card over to her.

'Oh my God,' she said, 'an original Picasso sketch. I can't really just take that, can I give you something for it?'

'No, that's okay,' said Picasso, wanting to get on with his coffee and newspaper.

'Oh, but I insist,' said the lady.

'Okay, give me 70,000 dollars,' said the maestro.

'What? 70,000 thousand dollars? But it took you only six seconds!'

'No, ma'am,' was the reply, 'it took me sixty years!'

I can't say it took me sixty years, but it took me the better part of ten years, between 1980 and 1991.

My parents would come twice a year to visit. I really looked forward to it, since besides their great love and support, one of the things most Indian mothers enjoy doing is cooking for their children. Though I could cobble together Indian dishes, my parents' tastes and culinary skills were the real thing!

Before they left, my mother would freeze containers of various curries for me. They would last me months and each time I defrosted and ate them I would miss them. My parents seemed so young and vital then, my dad wearing sunglasses while he chopped onions to stop his eyes watering, and my mom cooking up a storm.

Los Angeles is not necessarily a friendly place, especially if one is not successful, and if not exactly homesick, I often felt a deep longing for the familiarity of India and family and friends. In the 1980s, with no Indians in the entertainment business, it was a lonely, unforgiving spot. I used to recall my mother quoting from Henry Wadsworth Longfellow's 'The Ladder of St. Augustine' when she tried to encourage us to greater effort at tennis or at studies:

> *The heights by great men reached and kept*
> *Were not attained by sudden flight*
> *But they, while their companions slept,*
> *Were toiling upward in the night*

(When years later in 2010, *Variety* magazine did me the honour of celebrating my hundredth film with a special issue and a party in Cannes, I quoted this piece of inspiration.)

My feeling of isolation led me to go back to India for a break every now and then, perhaps twice a year. Then the restlessness would overtake me and I'd feel I had to get back to the grind and the risks of one disappointment after another, and I would return to LA, get back to work and once again look forward to my parents' visits.

One of the features of this to-ing and fro-ing between the continents was my chronic and acute air sickness. As mentioned earlier, I had suffered it as a young lad on my first flight and it had never relented or subsided.

As a Catholic I do believe that God and the will of God are present in the most minute affairs of our humble lives. I prayed for my air sickness, the bane of my younger days, to go.

I suppose there must have been some psychosomatic explanation for the sickness and this may be it: I realize today that as soon as I progressed in the movie business, realizing my ambitions, the air sickness began to recede and when I finally felt that I had arrived, this particular affliction was gone never to return. Okay, it may just be that it goes with age or there might be some other clinical explanation, but I am convinced it had something to do with the confidence that success gives you. It banishes forever the butterflies in the stomach.

I suppose a therapist might say – though I have never felt the need for one – (what? no shrink? and you say you live in LA? are you crazy?) that some deep insecurity, a sense perhaps of not being as charming or as talented as my beloved elder brothers undermined me and made me prone to debilitating air sickness. I cannot really verify the truth of that.

In 1984, on a trip to India, my parents made me an interesting proposition. My mother's business was doing very well. It could do with young blood from within the family and there were great prospects of expansion. My mother told me that her manufactured cartons were going all over the country and her firm, which literally began as a cottage industry, was beginning to export.

It was a prospect to consider. Yes, I was making films, small films, some of them only on video and some mainly seen in the darkest corners of Africa or pirated in Asia.

For someone else, the prospect of stepping out of the dream that had been mostly toil and trouble (and undoubtedly some fun) so far might have appealed. Here was a prosperous business which could only become more so. But the truth was that I wasn't even remotely tempted. I wanted to do what no Indian had done before – crack Hollywood wide open.

Another story: there was this guy who worked for the circus, cleaning up the arena after the elephants had done their act and maybe their thing, leaving deposits. There he was with his brush and pan every day. Over the long years the job gave him back trouble (more of my own back trouble later, though that wasn't elephants!) and when he'd recovered from the operation to cure it, the doctors suggested that he get another job. Maybe sitting at a desk and working at computers. Our hero was aghast. 'What? And give up showbiz?'

My parents' suggestion was a bit like that. I wasn't quite cleaning up after the elephants, but I wouldn't give up showbiz. I knew I would get that break, and I went back to LA. My parents may have been disappointed but they didn't stop me or attempt to stop me. They were, as always, totally supportive of my decision. They must have loved their children a lot to agree to all of them living away and apart in a different continent. There was no murmur of discouragement. We had to follow our own paths. A friend once said to me that I would only understand this unconditional love when I had my own kids. It's true. Even today, if I wake up earlier than usual and call my mother, her first question as she struggles with her ailments is, 'Why are you up so early? Is there something troubling you?'

BRINGING PRIYA HOME

I BEGAN THIS STORY by saying that 1990 will always count as the year that changed my life. While Hollywood has been known for a game of musical marriages where very many people change partners, for me 1990 was a year I made a life commitment. The movie that I made with Jean Claude, which was a breakthrough for my career and his, was the bonus.

My wife and I now came from India to LA. She was coming to my house for the first time, so I carried her over the threshold of what was then our Beverly Hills home. John (my ever-watchful and faithful major domo sent by my mom in 1988), who had taken charge of the house while I was away, was waiting for us.

I wondered how Chitra would react to America, to the house, to LA, to my friends, to my work commitments, to everything. I was frankly more than a little nervous about it. How would she react to these new surroundings, this new life? I was in familiar environs and had my routines of work and play, while she would be in a completely unfamiliar territory and would have to make a life from scratch. I hoped to support and help in any way I could, but I was in uncharted territory as well.

I tried to think back to the 1970s when I was first surrounded by a sea of unfamiliar white faces. I was to her still practically a stranger. After all we had got married just as we were getting to know each other, after spending perhaps ten hours in all together over the period of a few days.

In Chennai she had been surrounded by friends and, as girls and young women do, they had confided in each other and she lived with her parents, a very real social support. Had I induced her to leave her parents and come into a void?

As I knew all too well, LA could be a very lonely place and as I recall, the first year of our marriage was the most difficult. We had many soul-searching moments, and one of the things Chitra had to get her head around was that even though India was at the other end of the world, you could board a plane and go home. It would take twenty-four hours but you'd be there. I attempted to convince her that it wasn't exile, that I was starting to do well, and she had the wherewithal to fly back whenever she wanted. I knew though that she was the sort of person who would go to India only when it was convenient for my work.

Chitra started to formulate her own routines. She would go, accompanied by John, for walks. I undertook to teach her how to drive, since driving is something you have to do in LA if you are to acquire any kind of independence. But the instructor-learner relationship is such that I would recommend a professional driving school if encouraging your spouse to drive!

As she settled down and entered my very congenial and welcoming social circle, I felt she slowly started to feel less anxious. She wanted to be here. And when the first flush of unfamiliarity, loneliness and probably even wondering what the hell she had got herself into started to wane, things blossomed magically. It was our honeymoon period.

It was soon after we arrived in LA that I took Chitra to her

first Hollywood party at the home of Richard and Barbara Cohen
(Barbara was previously married to Cary Grant). The guests there
included Sidney Poitier, Zsa Zsa Gabor, Quincy Jones, Ringo
Starr and many other notables. It was a wonderful dinner and I
remember Chitra dressing up for it. She sat next to Zsa Zsa Gabor,
who said Chitra should have been an actress, and loved the sari and
all the accoutrements and jewellery that went with it.

On our first anniversary, we went to a restaurant called
L'Orangerie, which was in the heart of Beverly Hills and one of
the most sought after reservations at the time. We had a romantic
candle-lit dinner with champagne and some of my favourite red
wine. In the next couple of years, we entertained a lot at our home:
celebrities, studio executives, sports figures, and it was quite often
that a group of 35–40 people would be invited home for dinner.
Our dining room, living room and patio were all used for this
purpose. It was very much a couples' home, and we enjoyed every
minute that we spent there.

Our life together has taught me how to define love and while the
first thrill of meeting someone and the head-over-heels emotions
that accompanies it is wonderful, the steady growth of togetherness
is the real thing. I think of the way I met and married Chitra as
only technically an 'arranged marriage' – in reality it feels like it
was our destiny.

Just a few months after our marriage, Chitra handed me an
envelope, saying it had arrived that afternoon while I was out.
When you are a child, a letter in the mail box is one of the great
joys of life. Through your teens, each one is scrutinized and studied.
But at some point, letters become unimportant. Maybe it is the
avalanche of bills and bank statements that wear your joy away.

Or maybe it is the pace of life that makes you forget that you even have a letter.

But this one was different – it was from the Academy of Motion Picture Arts and Sciences, the august body that awards the Oscars each year, and it was addressed to me. I had been waiting with anticipation and some trepidation to see if my application to the Academy had been accepted.

The letter stated that the Academy had invited me to become its member – the first producer from India to be invited. My sponsors for the membership were Sherry Lansing, the president of 20th Century Fox, and Arnold Kopelson, the Academy Award-winning producer of *Platoon*.

It was 1992 and I was now a member of the Academy of Motion Pictures. I had been accepted by my peers!

I found myself driving to Charlton (Chuck) Heston's house on Benedict Canyon in Beverly Hills along with the ICM agent Jack Gilardi. Heston had been a childhood hero who I would watch during those incredible afternoons at Sapphire Theatre. After a casual and relaxed conversation about his career, I told him about watching *Ben Hur* as a boy in Chennai, about the impression it had made on me in those early days and about the response of the audience during the chariot race.

When I complimented him on his beautiful home, he said: 'You know, *Ben Hur* bought me this house.'

It was an exhilarating moment to have Chuck present me the plaque which read: 'Having demonstrated excellence in the Art, Science or Industry of the Motion Picture ...' He was full of praise, since he was a tennis fan and had watched my brothers and me play over the years.

Chuck and Lydia Heston remained friends of ours over the years. I've played tennis at Chuck's house and Chitra and I have enjoyed many afternoons and evenings with him and his lovely wife. Every year we got a Christmas card from them depicting a great scene from one of Chuck's extraordinary films. But as it must to all men, death came to Chuck on 5 April 2008. I was deeply saddened by his passing away.

In 1993 I was once again invited to Monaco for the Princess Grace charity event and going with Mrs Amritraj was truly idyllic. We decided to take my parents along, a dream of mine to reciprocate in some very small way what they had done for me. Prince Albert was a friend and he was charming to my wife and parents, as were Roger Moore and John Forsythe, amongst others. We went on from there to Venice, Florence and Rome. I recalled my first trip with my parents in 1971 although this one was first class all the way – Venetian gondolas, staying at the romantic Gritti Palace, the glory of the Vatican in Rome and the museums of Florence. On our return, we were elated to discover that Chitra was pregnant.

We decided to move to a larger house to accommodate our family-to-be. There were pangs at leaving the place where we had fallen in love, but it made sense to do so. Our child would be born; it would be a new adventure. As the poet Wordsworth says:

Though nothing can bring back the hour
Of splendour in the grass
Of glory in the flower
We shall grieve not, rather find
Strength in what remains behind ...

Or in this case, what we looked forward to.

So we left our lovely couples' retreat, and moved about ten minutes away to a much more spacious home set on two acres that included a tennis court, a swimming pool and a lovely hillside, all of which were surrounded by greenery including six beautiful oak trees. In October of 1993, we moved and awaited the arrival of our daughter Priya.

In January of 1994, we were awakened by a real jolt. The Northridge earthquake hit Los Angeles and was 6.7 on the Richter scale. LA is prone to quakes as it sits on the extremely dangerous San Andreas Fault. However, the damage to our home was minimal. I remember taking a pregnant Chitra, who had these sudden yearnings for food, to a doughnut shop that day and buying half-a-dozen doughnuts for her!

In May that year our daughter Priya was born. It was, as I think of it even now, a genetic coup. I had no sisters. Anand had a son and Vijay had two sons. When Chitra first told me that she was pregnant, I said we should without doubt expect a boy. It seemed to be, if not our destiny, then the family's fate. Some ancient spell perhaps that said, 'Bring forth male children only!'

After the first five months of her pregnancy, the doctor concluded after an ultrasound that it was certainly a boy. We started listing boys' names and began corresponding with both families for suggestions. Both our parents wanted an Indian name. Tom, Dick or Harry were definitely out! But one of the considerations is the difficulty that Americans have with pronouncing foreign names. I recalled how for many years, my name, simple though it may seem in its spelling, was massacred in pronunciation by my American friends. I knew of a Sikh in New York whose name was Jaswinder Singh and he used to be called 'Jazz Winder Singh'. Not a desirable fate, but he lived with it and eventually began introducing himself as 'Jazzy'. This is common with Indians living in the US who often shorten their names (like Siddharth to Sid).

So we determined that we'd find an Indian name that Americans could pronounce, one that rolled easily off the tongue. Then came the thunderclap or flash of lightning or whatever you like to call it. In month seven the ultrasound analyst told us, quite casually while perusing the data, 'Mm, it's a girl.'

'Come on,' I said, 'you're kidding, right?'

'No. Serious.'

'But we don't have girls in our family,' I said.

'You do now,' he said.

That was it. For just a little while, we panicked. Would we come up with a girl's name? Of course we would but the same criteria had to apply.

The choice came down to Maya and Priya, both pretty names derived from Sanskrit and meaning 'compassion' and 'love', and we chose love. Priya sounded right to us and for us.

We love it, and thank God for little girls. I had never been around them, but having a daughter and a son has been the greatest joy of my life.

Now my parents and Chitra's parents decided to come over to LA for the birth, and we thought that was great because neither of us had handled a birth before and all four of them were experienced hands, so I knew we'd get a lot of help.

They came and with them there the whole event turned out to be chaotic. I have never seen such chaos except perhaps on the set of *Jeans*! The family went overboard in their caring – outrageously, unhelpfully and, in the end, comically overboard. 'Is she ready to go to hospital?' was repeated fifty times a day. Everyone was on tenterhooks till finally the day arrived.

We got to Cedars Sinai, the famous hospital located in Beverly Hills that caters to the stars. Chitra's parents got lost in the complex of buildings that had complicated corridors. We had a delivery on our hands and two lost or missing Indians. My parents start panicking. We decided we should concentrate on the birth and finally, after a long labour, the baby was born. I cut the umbilical cord and when I held my daughter in my arms, I knew my life had changed forever. But there was an immediate problem. She emerged with fluid in her lungs. Watching her try to scream as a little suction bulb was inserted in her throat to squeeze out the fluid, I understood finally what it felt like to be a father.

This meant she had to be kept in the hospital to drain the fluid from her lungs. So we returned home without our new baby whom they kept in incubation for three days. I remember putting balloons all over the house as a welcome for the new mother. Since the baby was still in hospital, Chitra took one look at the balloons and started weeping. Pretty soon, both parents and I were crying as well.

The next day, we went to see the baby in the incubator. It was during visiting hours and our parents, as anxious as we were, came along. It was, for us as new parents, quite terrifying. Our parents' presence, with their concern and constant enquiries, made us more anxious. It was crazy. (Needless to say, for the birth of our second child, our son, we very diplomatically dissuaded any of them from coming over.)

Bringing the baby back home was memorable. I think that was the turning moment in Chitra's new life, from her fighting isolation to feeling at home in America. Now that she had our daughter, I could see the change clearly.

   And suddenly I noticed that my life had changed too. I remember my friends warning me against settling down, against getting married. They would say you're doing great, you have a beautiful house, you have a cook and most of all you have your freedom, no one to ask you where you're going, who you're going with, who you're bringing home, when you're coming back or anything. No accountability. Why put that noose around your neck?

   I'd reply that I'd done my freedom bit and enjoyed it, now I wanted to have a family. Freedom feels a lot like loneliness. Now after Priya was born, my friends said they could see the change. The child changed everything in our lives. There was no question of who wore the pants in our family. This little person in diapers ruled the roost.

   And she was, and continues to be, the only daughter and granddaughter in the Amritraj household!

   Talking of diapers, one day when she was a little more than a year old, Chitra was invited to a baby shower for the master chef Wolfgang Puck's son, which was hosted by Marciano, the owner of Guess Jeans. Chitra went to that lunch and left John, my Man Friday, and me in charge of Priya. Not realizing what I was getting into, I said it would be cool. I was boastfully confident.

   We went to the park with my daughter and were playing around. I have to admit to my shame that until that day I had never changed a diaper. And so yes, the moment arrived, Priya did what little girls do, and John and I were both dumbfounded. Like two civilians asked to diffuse a bomb. We did manage slowly, examining the pins and white cotton naturals that Chitra insisted on using, figuring out eventually how the wretched thing was to be removed.

I've seen the not-too-funny comic moment very many times in the movies before but being in the centre of it wasn't at all funny. I coped, did the whole thing with the baby equipment that Chitra had thoughtfully provided without instructions attached. Now folding and securing a diaper may not be rocket science but it's certainly geometry and I was never terribly good at that. We got the diaper functionally on, John handling the pins, but it wasn't how the experts do it, I was told later with all the hazards pointed out, which I will spare the reader.

The next big event was Priya's christening. The whole family, which means my brothers' families too, turned up. Anand was her godfather and Niranjali, Chitra's sister, was her godmother.

MILAN, COPPOLA AND
BOUNCY CASTLES

ON EVERY TRIP TO India I found myself being handed proposals for a Hollywood film in India, or for shooting an Indian film in the US or, more ambitiously, for making an Indian film that would work globally. Perhaps the birth of my daughter added to my nostalgia and I finally decided I was going to make an Indian film and, naturally, Tamil being my mother tongue, I decided to make it in Tamil. This would help continue my exploration of being a bridge between Hollywood and India, which had started many years ago with *Bloodstone* and Rajnikanth.

Through mutual friends I met this young director called Shankar who had done a couple of films, both in Tamil, both successes. I saw his films and proposed to him that he write and direct a film for me.

The actor we chose was not yet really an actor. Aishwarya Rai, who has gone on to be perhaps India's most famous actor, had just won the title of Miss World. What struck me when we first met was the combination of her self-assurance, enthusiasm and charm. I offered her the role and we started talking about money. Normally, in Hollywood, one talks to agents and lawyers about the deal. But here she was, wanting to conclude matters herself. So we walked to the corridor outside her suite, and for the first time in my life I was negotiating with an Indian actor. A young Indian girl, beautiful and without the least show of inhibition negotiating her own deal. I was amazed.

We made a deal, right there in the corridor. If it had been an agent, I might have bargained and both the agent and I would have started with an understanding of the terms and stratagems of such a negotiation, but she named a figure or asked me to name one. I went by what was fair and she agreed. It was weeks later that we did any paperwork and signed contracts and she didn't waver from what she had agreed to.

So Aishwarya was on board to do *Jeans*. We recruited a young Indian actor, Prashanth, to play the male lead. In Hollywood, unless you are making a musical, you think of the various other aspects of film-making first. In India, one starts thinking about the music almost before you have an idea for the script. We asked A.R. Rahman to do the music. AR was a music composer who had great success in the world of Indian cinema and subsequently won an Oscar for his music in *Slumdog Millionaire*.

At the time his career was just taking off. He had written and directed the music for one of India's dynamic directors, Mani Ratnam. AR, though very much in demand, readily agreed. He has become a good friend.

Perhaps because I was from Hollywood and didn't have the cunning which Indian producers use to cut corners and costs, *Jeans* turned out to be the most expensive film made at the time. One day, our director Shankar came to me and said he wanted to shoot one song using the background of all the seven wonders of the world. Right! That made me think. We were already shooting forty-five days in India and forty-five days in the US. Shankar wanted to go all round the world to shoot this one song? There were other ways, I said.

I told him that when we got to LA we'd go across to Warner Brothers and using a sound stage put up a green screen, shoot second unit at the locations to get us the actual background (or plates, as they are called) and voila, we'd get our actors at the seven wonders of the world. But Shankar wasn't satisfied. He said, 'Please let me know the budget you can give me to shoot on location.'

There was something in what he said about the quality on screen in these earlier days of VFX and what you couldn't do with green screen and what you could do with being there. So having agreed on the budget I gave him, we ended up going to the seven wonders of the world, globe-trotting from the pyramids of Egypt to the Great Wall of China, the Eiffel Tower, the Taj Mahal and others, for just one song.

The crew was talented and very hard working, without complaints and restraints, and as a small thank you, while we were shooting a song in the Grand Canyon, I flew in idlis and sambar and all kinds of South Indian dishes from the Gandhi Restaurant in Las Vegas as a surprise for the cast and crew. Needless to say, we had an even more productive few days after that.

Jeans, my only Indian-language film, released in 1997, was one of the Tamil industry's biggest hits. Rahman's music was phenomenal and topped the charts for a long time. *Jeans* was for many years a record-holding film in South India – till Rajni's next movie came around.

Back in LA, one of the signs of the success of my career was the Saturday tennis games moving to my home tennis court. It is a game that is on the must-go-to list. Studio and agency heads, along with various stars, directors and producers, at one point or another, has played at my home. They would show up and we would play sets from 10 a.m. to about 1 p.m. On some days this would be followed by lunch, which would be either catered, or put together by Chitra, who had become very adept at the art of entertaining. It was overall an enjoyable morning of tennis and conversation. It makes me think back to those days when I was lucky to be invited to the homes of Tom Laughlin and others, and I couldn't help but feel that a big circle had been closed and while I was and always will be a Wimbledon tennis player, I certainly had become one of the producer elite in Hollywood.

Good relationships in Hollywood are as important as good wine. My tennis mornings as well as the projects over the last two decades have brought me into contact with many major studio executives, stars and agency heads, and I must say that those relationships I built up have stood me in extremely good stead.

My Hollywood tennis-playing friends also supported my philanthropic pursuits. From the year 2001 onwards, I decided to organize a charity tennis event at the Riviera Country Club, which was one of the posh clubs in Los Angeles. It was to benefit the Children's Hospital in LA which did admirable work in providing free medical care for parents who could not afford it for their children. The choice of charity was a thank you for being lucky enough to have two healthy children of my own.

Each September, I would hold an event that started with a dinner for the participants on a Saturday night at one of the top hotels – the Beverly Wilshire. Each company – studios, networks and other production and technology companies – would pay $10,000 for a table at the event. I would then do the draw for the tennis tournament the next day where thirty-two players would make up sixteen teams, and they would play against each other.

It was very important that I did the draw as to who was partnering with whom in front of all of the people, so it did not look like it was rigged, which in Hollywood it could be or would be for all sorts of professional and political purposes and as a means of advancing this or that person.

So one has to be very careful, as who partners with who is as important as who does not partner with a person he or she detests. However, in this particular case, it was complete chance as to who your partner would be, and I must say, it made for many exciting and tantrum-filled moments for the five years that I ran the event. Certain years, two weeks before the event, I would get calls from chairmen of studios or agencies about who they did not want to be paired with. 'Hey Ashok, please don't pair me with that ass ...' was the tenor of some of these diplomatic calls!

By 2006, the event got more difficult to produce than some of my movies, considering the personalities involved, and I decided that since I had raised a few million dollars for the Children's Hospital, it was time to bring the event to an end.

When you play tennis you either win or you lose – it's black and white – but the movie business is a grey area. I don't think anyone can quite predict if a movie's going to be a big hit or a flop. The economics of the industry are constantly changing. It's not the kind of business where you're making chocolates or shoes. Movies are not an assembly line. It's how you package this and what you do with that, your relationship with the studio, and it's also about how and when the movie is released. So many good movies don't get a proper release. On the other hand, studios spend $50 million on prints and advertising on so many films that don't seem to deserve it. Against this backdrop I set out to produce smart, creative, independent films with Academy Award-winning actors and directors.

For me, it always starts at a creative level. I first have to be passionate about the screenplay. I then check with my international division and see how it works for them, as well as with the domestic distributors in terms of its domestic potential. I then check with the talent agencies to see what level of talent the project can attract. Once I've figured all that out, then it's a question of 'what level of talent' based on 'what level of budget'. If I have a major director or star, I want to make sure we have domestic distribution in place, whereas if I'm making a movie for $10 million, then I have more freedom with the kind of talent and material we choose.

I've always maintained a close relationship with the actors and directors I've worked with, both the experienced ones and the new talent. It's terrific to work creatively with them in crafting a film and watching it come together.

An actor I was keen on working with was Ben Kingsley, having visited the set of *Gandhi* a decade before and having watched him perform so incredibly, bringing that character to life and in the process winning the Academy Award.

I read the script for *The Confession*. At my request Ben Kingsley and Alec Baldwin, who today has become quite an iconic television figure with the hit show *30 Rock*, agreed to star in the film. Amy Irving, who was at that time married to Steven Spielberg, rounded out a stellar cast, and the film, which was a dramatic character piece, is one I'm quite proud of.

~⊷⊶~

Chitra and I had more wonderful news. We had been trying for a second child and were informed that Chitra was pregnant. It would be a boy. This was thrilling. It would make the family complete and the balance of genders seemed God's gift, though neither Chitra nor I were in the least concerned about gender. The months of pregnancy were anxious in a pleasant way. Waiting for the birth was watching the completion of a cycle of the miracle.

Our son was, the doctors determined, to be born through Caesarean section. We chose the date, and on 20 February 1998, he came into this world, two days before my birthday and as I later found out, on the same day as my friend Sidney Poitier was born seventy years earlier. We again went through the task of picking names, and this time came up with an unusual one: Milan, which means 'union' in Sanskrit. We had once again kept in mind our parents' approval as well as something easy for the Western palate. It has worked.

After the operation Chitra had to stay on in hospital. I have never seen her happier, because she could be with Milan at her choosing. The doctors had minor concerns about her recovery, so they would take the baby from her on and off and bring him back to her when she wanted him.

In the mid-to-late nineties, I was working at an incredible pace: *The Confession* was in production, *Jeans* was in successful release and my next films were ready to roll. *Boondock Saints* was regarded as one of the hottest scripts in Hollywood. Troy Duffy, the writer/ director, indicated that the screenplay was inspired by personal experience while living in Los Angeles. Harvey Weinstein, who headed Miramax at that time, made a deal with him and, in fact, gifted him a bar – meaning a place where people serve drinks – in order to acquire this screenplay. However, later, there was a fallout between Harvey and Troy, and the screenplay came loose.

I remember the Christmas party at my home where Troy came along with a small entourage and where we discussed his screenplay and subsequently greenlit the picture. Incidentally, talent agents have a habit of blowing smoke up one's ass when they have a moment of success. Some artists can handle this, and others can't. Shooting commenced in Toronto, with the final scenes being filmed in Boston, and the movie went on to become a cult hit on DVD and late-night showings, not unlike the *Rocky Horror Picture Show*. As it happens, Troy Duffy suffers in painful obscurity – another casualty of Hollywood.

The Christmas party itself was memorable for other reasons.

We had invited, amongst others, several friends who had children our kids' age. We'd contracted an act of a Santa Claus and an elf to help Santa with his presents, and we had a bouncy castle set up in the garden along with a pony ride through the front and rear of our house.

As the evening progressed, I could see that Santa Claus and the elf were a little unsteady on their feet, I further observed them taking a little nip out of a bottle from their pockets. I realized that they had drained their bottles of Scotch and were getting smashed during the process of laughing and talking with the parents and kids. Pretty soon, the elf trotted across and fell on our sidewalk. It was not a very pleasant sight and while I was tending to the elf, the bouncy castle deflated and the kids were trapped inside. So I jumped in and pulled out all the kids. Nothing serious happened or could have happened – after all the fabric was plastic and rubber – but it was nerve-wracking. I don't suppose any of the parents or kids have been to a party quite like that before or since and they certainly haven't stopped talking about it.

The Third Miracle starring Ed Harris and Anne Heche was a film of mine that held particular interest. It had the legendary director of *The Godfather*, Francis Ford Coppola, as its executive producer.

The Coppola family is extremely talented, with Francis at the helm, his nephew Nicolas Cage (the star of one of my recent films, *Ghost Rider: Spirit of Vengeance*) on the one hand, and his daughter Sofia Coppola, a writer/director on the other. His father, Carmine Coppola, is a terrific composer and his sister, Talia Shire, and her son, Jason Schwartzman, who also did a movie for me called *Shopgirl* some years later, are versatile actors. What a family they are. Overall, I can say I have worked with and had fun moments with most of the Coppola family.

Besides making some of the best films in Hollywood, Francis had created his own vineyard. As you may recall from an earlier chapter, I had become a huge fan and aficionado of red wine, and the Coppola vineyard in northern California's Napa Valley can boast some of the finest wines in the country. A few years later, when Talia Shire, who also played the wife of Sly Stallone in *Rocky*, came to my house for dinner, she brought along a case of the Coppola wine and since then I have developed a great liking for his wines.

Finally, there was *Get Carter* with Sylvester Stallone on board. Sly and I had many interesting conversations on set about the way he had broken into the industry and comparisons with how I had done the same. He is a gentleman and a professional with a great understanding of every aspect of the movie industry.

Looking back at my films of the 1990s, I came of age as a creative producer, learning to work with Oscar-winning actors and directors, not being intimidated by stars or studio names, and understanding the necessity to be involved in every aspect of film-making, from the inception to the time it hit the screen.

In 1998, back in India, *Jeans* was India's selection by the Film Federation of India for the Foreign Film Academy Award. Incidentally, from 1994 onwards for many years, I was honoured to serve on the board for foreign films at the Academy of Motion Pictures (the first Indian to have done so). In 2002, I was also invited to join the British Academy Board in Los Angeles, and the International Council for the Emmy Awards. It was the first time (at least to my knowledge) that any producer, let alone an Indian, was on all three of these prestigious boards simultaneously.

Ironically, that same year came the onslaught of my acute back problem. I had severe and constant pains but they got very acute in May of 1998 when I was returning from the Cannes Film Festival. The diagnosis was that part of my vertebral column, the meniscus between the discs at L4 and L5, and L5 and S1 had completely disintegrated, which in layman's terms means that when you look at the MRI scan, the x-ray as it were, you see a big black mark where there should be spongy meniscus separating the bones. Bone scraping bone is what causes the pain. There is no easy solution.

It was my most miserable Cannes festival. I didn't need a doctor to tell me that it was all those years of tennis and the extraordinary stress of learning to balance family with business both in the US and India that had worn me out mentally and physically. This time, on the way back, I was in excruciating pain at the airport in Nice. They had to take me to the plane in a wheelchair. I had to get to Frankfurt for my connecting flight to LA.

My parents came to pick me up at the airport only to see me being wheeled off the plane again. At the hospital in LA, at first, I couldn't even lie flat on my back long enough for an MRI scan so that the doctors could find out exactly what was wrong. Instead they had to take repeated x-rays. They suggested cortisone shots in my spine to relieve the pain, which it did for a while, but then the pain came back.

All through that year, and most memorably through Milan's

christening and the party after (Vijay was Milan's godfather and Helen, Anand's wife, was his godmother), I was either in a wheelchair or on crutches. And I came close to having surgery on my back. Several people warned me against it. Many specialists told me that there were two ways that the operation on my spinal column could be performed. They could go in through the abdomen, move the intestines out of the way and replace the disintegrated discs. The other option was to fuse the discs together and insert steel rods on either side of the discs. Either way they said the chances of success were 50:50 and that surgery could lead to further damage to the spine. I decided against it.

Instead I was given a regimen of workouts. I do the exercises every day. A combination of praying to Our Lady of Velankanni and strengthening the muscles this way seems to have worked to an extent, but I still have to be extremely careful.

HYDE PARK IN HOLLYWOOD

THE FASCINATION OF FLIGHT can't be expressed in words. Crossing the Atlantic in the luxury of a Gulfstream 5 private jet from London to Los Angeles, I was looking out of the window to very pure and fine clouds, and below us lay the vast Atlantic Ocean. For human eyes to see all this enlarges the horizon as the world from above seems so beautiful and spiritual. Crossing the pond had become a normal feature in modern-day aviation and I too had begun to enjoy travelling by air after my initial fears as a child. On that flight I was thinking about the changes taking place in my life.

It was time for Priya to go to kindergarten. I remember the first day Chitra and I dropped her at school. The banner read: 'Class of 2012'. Being forty-four years old at that time, 2012 felt a long way off. I hoped I would not be watching her graduate high school while I was on a walker. Milan was a year old and as Chitra and I marvelled at his first steps, the whole Amritraj family gathered for my parents' fiftieth wedding anniversary. It was truly golden.

(Priya is now in college, and boy, has the time gone fast ... and I'm not on a walker!)

On the business side, as I had anticipated, studios were starting to co-finance many of their motion pictures with producers who had the proven (and that, in ninety-nine out of a hundred cases, meant box-office) ability to develop, produce and co-finance major motion pictures. This ability to do all of the above separated the producers who waited for a decision 'hat in hand' from the ones who were able to be on equal footing and garner the proper attention of the studios. I wanted to be one of the latter kind.

In February 1999, right after my birthday, this led to the creation of my biggest venture, which I named Hyde Park Entertainment. How did the name suggest itself? Many years previously, when I played tennis at Wimbledon in London, I would walk around in Hyde Park and spend meditative and enjoyable afternoons there. Those who know London and its changeable but ultimately seductive and charming weather (yes, okay, it can be a nuisance when it's grey and drizzly) regard the park as a central cultural heritage. I took its name. For the animated logo of the firm, I decided on another iconic London landmark, Tower Bridge, which spans two shores, the north and south, reflecting my personality and my ambition, which was always to span the two cultures into which I was born and which I had adopted. So with a name and logo in place it was time to get started.

The first step was to construct an overall deal with one or two studios. A 'first-look deal', as it is called, is one where a producer is contracted to present his projects first to a certain studio, in return for which the studio not only looks at the project quickly and in a positive light, but at the same time also pays for the privilege of doing so.

A 'second-look deal' is exactly what it sounds like – when the first-look studio passes, one is then obliged to go to the second-look studio in a similar manner. Obviously, the producer thinks that the rejection from the first-look studio is something that those gentlemen (and sometimes ladies) will come to regret when the film is made and goes into stratospheric orbit, but that's the difference between an initiating producer's passion and the cold calculations of the studio.

To have a first-look deal in 1999 was quite sought after as there were only twenty to thirty such deals made by each studio who were petitioned by thousands of producers for them. For one to have a first-look and second-look deal was rare and if you had both, you would be among the top producers in Hollywood.

That's an exclusive club considering that all the world is pushing at every door in Hollywood.

The people who represented Hyde Park now were a far cry from those who had tried to help Amritraj Productions in those early days. Twenty years of blood, sweat and some salty tears were responsible for bringing in the new relationships, the know-how and the irresistible clout. Skip Brittenham, one of the most powerful, if not the most powerful lawyer in town, and Arnold Rifkin, then president of the William Morris Agency, represented Hyde Park.

Now with Skip and Arnold aboard we made appointments and went in turn to the seven major studios in Hollywood. They are known as the Seven Sisters after the cluster of stars called the Pleiades. In Greek mythology each of the seven is pursued by the gods, so I suppose we were cast in that role, pursuing deals with the heads of each. It did not hurt that Skip Brittenham probably represented most of them, and Arnold dealt with them every day. I, of course, at this point, was a producer of some renown, having had a decade of success. However, the huge hit was not yet in place though there was every promise it would come. Success breeds success – if you're lucky.

In October of 1999, we decided on the two studios that we

would make our deals with. The first-look deal was to be with MGM – the fabled studio of *Gone with the Wind*, *Rocky*, the James Bond films, and the great musicals of years past. The studio had new management – Alex Yemenijian was chairman and Chris McGurk (who was part of my Saturday tennis game) was vice-chairman, and the owner of the studio was the legendary Kirk Krekorian, who had bought and sold it three times. He was now once again its owner.

My second-look deal was with the Walt Disney Studios, which was of course created by the extraordinary talent of Walt Disney and was run by Joe Roth, a former producer and a talented and powerful studio executive.

After heated negotiations, we closed Hyde Park's first and second-look deals, and I became one of the few producers in town to have attained this status. Certainly, there was no Indian or Asian producer anywhere in Hollywood who had these deals. In such a competitive industry with its share of show-offs, and with the press and public dedicated to gathering the gossip and examining the minutiae of everything, very little remains a secret.

Hyde Park opened its office doors at the MGM lot in Santa Monica. I had realized in 1990 that the international market was of critical importance, and would be, in fact, the key growth area in the decades to come. Today it is two-thirds of the world box office. Over the past two decades I have focused much of my energy to learning and developing my international network of contacts.

My movies from the 1990s had performed well internationally, and as such, almost every distributor had made significant sums of money off my films. So in 1999, when I went around to the foreign distributors to structure output deals, I got a warm reception. I should explain: an output deal is where a territory like Germany or Italy enters into a deal with a major producer whereby the distributor pre-buys all the films produced by the producer before they are made and contributes the purchase price, a percentage of the budget, to it. Obviously, the distributor has to have a lot of faith in the producer as he is paying for a slate of films without knowing how they will turn out. He is backing the horse and jockey before they are on the turf.

One of the major international companies that had just been formed was a partnership between Leo Kirch (Kirch Media), perhaps the most successful entertainment figure in Germany, and Silvio Berlusconi (the former prime minister of Italy) whose company Mediaset was a powerhouse in Italy. Together they formed a company called Epsilon, which was operating all through Europe.

They decided to make a deal with a couple of top Hollywood producers. I was one of them. I entered into an output deal with Epsilon for five years, wherein Epsilon would acquire the European rights for any movie that Hyde Park and I produced. It was an extremely lucrative deal, and as I look back, groundbreaking in its structure.

In hand now was my first-look deal with MGM, my second-look deal with Disney and my European deal with the conglomerate Epsilon. I was ready to make movies.

In November 1999, one night I received a phone call from Arnold Rifkin. 'Ashok,' he said, 'I'd really like you to read this script called *Bandits* right away – it's on its way to your home.'

'Sure,' I said, 'I'll definitely read it, but what's the urgency?'

'Bruce Willis is the urgency,' he said, or words to that effect. 'Bruce is in. He wants to do it.'

Arnold didn't have to remind me that Bruce had just made a

universal hit with *The Sixth Sense*. Bruce was, in the temperature metaphor that Hollywood adopted if not invented, 'hot' (and I subsequently discovered how 'cool' he was at the same time.)

Arnold was Bruce's agent as well as mine and he told me that he had already sent the script to Joe Roth, who was then chairman of Disney Studios. He wasn't setting up a competition, as some agents on occasion do, offering the same script to rivals simultaneously and challenging them to take part in an auction, but providing me an early look at a key project because of our relationship.

I got the script and read it that night. I called him at 8 a.m. the next morning and said it was a great script and that I was very enthusiastic about doing it.

'That's great because Joe read it and he's in!'

Rarely do major movies come together so smoothly, and I was waiting for the surprise. 'Joe says he'll do the movie as long as it costs under $60 million,' he said.

Joe confirmed to me that that was his limit on this one.

Enter Skip Brittenham, Bruce Willis's lawyer (and as I said earlier, mine as well). Skip began the negotiations on Bruce's behalf. Representing both the buyer and the seller of talent is walking a tightrope. The element of bargaining gets suspended because you can't bargain on both sides. The deal has to be accepted on perceptions of a fair market value for the talent on offer.

Skip ended up negotiating a $22 million deal for Bruce.

This took the budget, considering that there were other actors to be contracted – after all, the movie was called 'Bandits' and not 'Bandit' – to over $60 million.

Tough!

True to Joe Roth's stated and non-negotiable limit, Disney withdrew from the deal. They wouldn't play.

Arnold and I, with Skip still acting for both parties, then took the project to MGM, where Alex Yemenidjian was chairman and Chris McGurk (another Skip client) was vice-chairman. They read the script, were very excited about Bruce Willis and said they wanted to do the movie at whatever price. Obviously the sky wasn't the limit, but they didn't specify a ceiling as Joe had.

We were now informed that Bruce Willis had been introduced to the script by Val Kilmer and they had a tacit agreement, as actors often do on their informal network, to both star in it. Alex and Chris were told that the deal would include Val Kilmer and they thought about it and came back saying quite emphatically that they did not want Val in it and would only do the movie if we could find a way around this.

This was a very tough call. We wanted to make this movie and that meant calling up Val Kilmer's agent, Creative Artists Agency (CAA), the most powerful agency in town, and telling them that Val was out.

A further complication came to light. Val Kilmer, a talented actor, was legally represented by none other than Skip Brittenham. I could see the trap that was closing in on me. Val's agent and another senior executive of CAA told me that if I didn't include Kilmer in *Bandits*, I could never work with CAA again. They would blacklist my productions. Seeing as they were at the time, and continue to be, the most powerful agency representing talent, this was not a very palatable prospect. I dared not even call it a threat!

MGM had drawn their line in the sand and were unwilling to cross it. CAA insisted on our casting Val. I knew that Val Kilmer had no contractual or legal right to be starring in the movie. He had introduced the script to Bruce Willis as a friend. However, that was not the way the script and the deal had reached me.

At the end of the day, I decided to make the movie and I told CAA that, however regrettable, the studio wouldn't cast Val and so unfortunately he was out.

I approached, with MGM's approval, Barry Levinson, who read the script and was happy to direct.

We then contracted Billy Bob Thornton to play the second lead role with Bruce and at the same time approached Academy Award winner Cate Blanchett. This was a dream cast with an Oscar-winning director.

CAA may have been serious about their threat, but it didn't last. I made up with them when casting their actor-clients in a subsequent film and all was well. Why? At the end of the day, I was here to stay, making movies, and because in an industry like Hollywood, the temptations of profit are more alluring than the sanctions of revenge.

Bandits was MGM's biggest movie of the year, and the premiere party that MGM had at Spago, one of the top restaurants in LA, was one where roads in Beverly Hills were shut down (not easy to do), and Spago and its surroundings from Canon Drive to Rodeo Drive were tented. It was a party that was, to that date, one of a kind. MGM's premieres and after-parties, in large part due to Jamie McGurk (Chris' wife), were some of the best parties in Hollywood.

Bandits got made in mid-2001 and we were very proud of it. Barry Levinson, who had previously directed the Oscar-winning *Rain Man*, was finishing the post-production and MGM had scheduled the release for October that year. Then something unforeseen happened.

On 9/11 I was in my home in Los Angeles, and I remember

getting a call from a friend at the Hollywood trade paper *Variety*, saying, 'You should turn on the TV set and hear what's happening.' The news talked of the catastrophic attack on the Twin Towers in New York. It was with a feeling of disbelief that people in America and around the world watched, but I don't think at that moment anyone knew how much each of our lives would change and how much the world would be affected by that one incident.

The world changed. The United States was wounded.

In Los Angeles, most of the TV and film studios went dark on action and comedy. It was considered painful to make action the theme of mere entertainment when the country had suffered the reality of it. The US was, for once, the victim of a terror raid and it was thought distasteful, at least for a while, to carry on laughing as we used to before the catastrophe.

As far as MGM was concerned, everything was set for the release of *Bandits* and they could not or would not change the release date, move it back till the period of national mourning had somewhat faded and the bruise to the nation's pride was allowed time to heal. MGM and Hyde Park had co-financed the film, but MGM had the call on the US release date. After much discussion, *Bandits* opened in October. It seemed a crazy thing to do. The attack on Iraq was under debate and the studio could have perhaps held the release. But they went ahead.

Despite the national mood, *Bandits* found its audience and the movie grossed $69 million. In any other circumstance and season there is no question it would have made a great deal more. *Bandits* also garnered various awards, including two Golden Globe nominations.

From 2000 onwards, the start of the new millennium, my wife and I decided to introduce Hollywood to the Diwali celebrations that we enjoyed so much during our growing years in India. Each year since we would take over a fancy Indian restaurant, decorate it and invite a bunch of close friends. I think I've introduced more Westerners to Indian food over the last thirty years, single-handedly, than anyone else. Our celebration has grown in the last decade and an invitation to these select Indian 'festival of lights' parties is, I am told, through either hints or plain pestering, much sought after.

While I was going through the *Bandits* saga, Chris McGurk, who had become a close friend, asked me if I was interested in partnering with MGM on a movie they were making called *Original Sin*. The chairman of MGM, Alex Yemenijian, was very passionate about this film. The writer/director was Michael Cristofer, who had made a film called *Gia* which had won a Golden Globe for Angelina Jolie. She was starting to come into prominence and had been cast in the lead role of a movie called *Lara Croft: Tomb Raider*.

I remember sitting with Chris McGurk when she walked into the office. We were blown away. She was beautiful, interesting, smart and passionate about the film. The lead actor, who was a bigger star at that point, was Antonio Banderas, who I was working with for a second time, having done a movie with him some years prior. I agreed to co-finance the picture and co-produce it with MGM, and we decided to go with Angelina Jolie for the pivotal female role. Angie was terrific in the film, as was Antonio Banderas.

The movie came out in 2001. The censors rated it 'R' for the theatres — 'R' for 'restricted', meaning theatres could only admit moviegoers seventeen years of age or older — but with the addition of deleted scenes, the DVD was unrated (meaning the censors had not given this version a rating), making the DVDs fly off the shelves.

In 2001 I was invited to judge the Miss World contest in Sun City in South Africa. Now which red-blooded male (or female for that matter) would turn that down? Let's just say judging the event over a few days was an interesting experience. On the last day, as I was departing, I remember seeing a young Indian girl waiting for her car. Mine had arrived a little earlier. I asked her if she wanted a lift. We drove together to the airport, and she introduced herself as Priyanka Chopra, the winner of the previous year's Miss World. She had come there to crown the new winner.

She mentioned that she was in the process of entering the Hindi film industry, and asked if I could give her any pointers. If memory serves me right, I told her that every actor, director and producer faces constant rejection and she would need to have faith in herself while showing the industry what makes her unique. It has been a pleasure to note the great success she has had over the past decade and see what a true star she has become.

In 2002, Dick Cook, the head of marketing at Disney, took over the Walt Disney Company as its chairman. Joe Roth had moved on, Hyde Park's deal was renewed under the new regime, and I made my next film with Disney called *Moonlight Mile*. It was a heartfelt film and reading the script I decided that it would bring the company, the team and, of course, me as a film-maker critical acclaim. It would be a conscious deviation into the non-commercial, though not right into the arty avant-garde film sector. I was thinking of American, not French critics!

I began work with the writer/director Brad Silberling. He wanted to tell an almost autobiographical story with extraordinary feeling and touching moments. It was extremely gratifying and at the same time humbling when Brad was quoted in *Variety* as saying: 'He reminds me a lot of how Steven Spielberg always described the now-late David Brown, because Ashok is like this incredibly stylish ambassador on behalf of the film-maker, a combination of real old world patron and true defender of the work.'

The script was truly inspiring and fresh and when we had Dustin Hoffman read it, he thought the same and agreed to star in it. Susan Sarandon and Jake Gyllenhaal, who was early in his career and not yet the star he is now, joined the cast. We also introduced Ellen Pompeo who has gone on to become a big TV star with *Grey's Anatomy*.

I had seen *The Graduate* when I was still in India, and now working with Dustin Hoffman was exciting. He was a huge tennis fan, with one of the few clay courts in LA at his home. We played often, both at his home and mine.

Overall *Moonlight Mile* ended up winning several awards in various festivals and vindicated my ambition to make a film which would be more artistic and win critical acclaim. We premiered at the Toronto Film Festival. Disney released it in the US, and with my European partners we released it internationally.

So in 2002, between *Original Sin*, *Bandits* and *Moonlight Mile*, the biggest stars were working with me at Hyde Park.

More importantly, the same year my daughter Priya won her first trophy for the under-eight singles in tennis.

From the time Priya was about five years old, I used to take her out to our backyard onto the tennis court, and from the time she was seven, for the next four to five years, on weekends, we would go to small towns like Anaheim, Ventura, Santa Barbara and others, about an hour outside of LA, to little clubs or public courts where Priya would play in the United States Tennis Association's (USTA) official tournaments in the under-eight, under-ten and subsequently in the under-twelve.

Each weekend I would wake Priya up at about six in the morning, we would go out and practise through her tears (she never wanted to wake up so early on a Saturday and Sunday!) and then we would change, I would bundle her into the car, and we would drive off to the tournament. In the car we would listen to my favourite mix tape of the Beatles, the Beach Boys, Celine Dion and Frank Sinatra, and I think Priya fell in love with Beatles during these trips, and still enjoys listening to them.

We would go to the tournament, she would play her match, and every now and then, she would have to go to the bathroom. I must say the bathrooms at those public courts were rather scary, so I would go into the ladies' room with her and sort of stand with my back to the door, making sure no one else was in there or could go in. I was petrified that there was a back door, or that some weird stranger would be wandering about. I think most parents would identify with that sort of worry, especially at lonely restrooms.

It was clear that Priya had some talent for the game, though both Chitra and I weren't sure she should take this up as a profession as her father and uncles had done. We finally decided when she was twelve that professional tennis was not for her. She was good, but it wasn't going to be her life, and professional tennis would also, we were certain, disrupt her studies. Of course tennis is in the blood and the family culture, and we wanted her to continue playing. She has proudly represented her school, Campbell Hall, as part of the team that was the unbeaten Division I champions in California, and she currently plays for her college.

I should mention as well that my son Milan plays for the boys' tennis team at Campbell Hall. Clearly tennis is written into my children's DNA. The nature-nurture debate takes on a new challenge! Even at a very young age Milan was confident on the tennis court and, in fact, today he excels in speech and debate, winning tournaments as he represents his school and speaks to audiences. I might have had a hand in that confidence.

Milan has been a part of the student council in his school, and he's very much about being an organizer and has tremendous leadership qualities. However, when it comes to writing a speech, he turns to his dad. So, yes, I have become a Milan speechwriter. For the past four years – sixth, seventh, eighth and ninth grades – I've written each of his speeches, and I must admit we are a sensational combination, as those speeches won him a position in the student council – the final one being a couple of months ago as I write this book, in high school, where only one boy was chosen from his grade. Writing those speeches and discussing them with Milan has really been something that's brought us close.

Managing the demands of work and family is something most people understand (thank God Chitra took on so much of the heavy lifting when it came to the kids), but still there are always conflicts and a delicate balance that I tried hard to maintain. Let me illustrate the dilemma with one incident where I made the wrong decision.

2006 was an extremely busy year for me. I was coming out of the production of *Shopgirl* and *Dreamer*. While the past decade or more had been quite crazy, this was a particularly trying time as I was dealing with different studios. *Shopgirl* was at Disney, *Dreamer* was at Dreamworks, and I had been presented this project, *Premonition*, over which we were in negotiations with Sony. So when Cannes of 2006 came up, I felt I had to attend in order to deal with the studios as well as foreign buyers, and I also needed to get a certain number of international sales to put *Premonition* into production.

Unfortunately, May of 2006 happened to be when Milan was

having his first holy communion, on a date fixed by the church. It fell during the first few days of the Cannes Film Festival which I could not miss that year. I had to make a choice – I went to Cannes. If I was to think of one specific moment that made it clear that my work came ahead of my family when it should not have, that was perhaps it.

While I had already attained a great deal of success since 1991 and *Double Impact*, I had not consciously put my work in second position to my family, and I think this one event gnawed away at my conscience so much that even though my family had always been critically important – we had our spring trips together, etc. – this event and the residual feeling of unease cleared up things for me once and for all. Since then family has taken the priority position, though if I am honest I have to keep reminding myself of the ratio.

It's now a cliché, the work:home or career:kids balance. The meditation on this theme, or the constant nagging of it, made me come to at least one conclusion. In a business like mine where Hollywood consumes your life, especially when success burdens you with more and more work and responsibility, one should make sure the balance between family and business is discussed. Talk about it. Be open about it. Debate it, come to conclusions about what each of you do rather than duck and dive and try and be in two places at once.

⚜

I have always hired and nurtured good executives at Hyde Park who have gone on to terrific careers. One such executive was Todd Lieberman who was a VP at my company. He knew a young writer called Jason Filardi who was starting his career then but is now very successful and in the high earner bracket of Hollywood writers.

He approached us with an idea which we picked up and took to MGM. On hearing the idea and reading the outline, MGM decided to pass on it and to this day regret their decision. We then took it to Disney under our second-look deal. At Disney they liked the concept, and we developed the screenplay. The idea was at the time titled 'Jail Bait'.

The story was a classic comedy that actually was a vehicle for a middle-aged Caucasian star and a younger, mid-thirties' African-American actress. The fact that it was a comedy that needed a particular style immediately made us think of Queen Latifah, the singer-actor. She heard the idea, read the screenplay and came on board; she was ideal for the role. It was destined, if not written for her.

Then we approached Steve Martin who joined us. This was my first outing with Steve and my first experience of his remarkable talent. Over the years I had watched him on the TV show *Saturday Night Live* and he is terrific.

The director was a young man who had made just one film prior to this one. His name was Adam Shankman. (Adam has since become one of the most sought after comedy directors, making films like the worldwide hit *Hairspray*.)

We titled our film *Bringing Down the House*, and the picture went into production with Disney. *House* was blessed with a team of gifted comic talents. Steve, Queen Latifah and Eugene Levy worked wonders within the framework of the screenplay, but when your cast is as naturally funny as these three actors, one should always let them play around with the dialogue a bit. Sometimes the funniest jokes in a film with this kind of comic pedigree are the ones that the actors improvise on the spot. The final film ended up as a combination of the original screenplay and the cast's brilliant improvisations. Other funny moments had to be left on the cutting room floor. It was one of the most enjoyable movies I've made, and one of the most interesting combinations of stars and director.

In the process of making commercial films in Hollywood, we cut the film, finish it and then preview it to audiences. It's what the industry calls a research screening. A company called National Research Group (NRG) did the screening for *Bringing Down the House*. The audience is a deliberately mixed sample consisting of men and women, African-Americans, Caucasians, Latinos and other minorities, all chosen to fall into the age categories of under and over twenty-five. The audience are then given a questionnaire and asked to score the movie in several ways which may indicate to us how the national audience will react.

In one of these trials for *Bringing Down the House*, we scored extremely high across the board because we insulted everybody uniformly in the movie. The script and gags laughed at every race and creed. The only thing which the audience felt could be better was the ending.

Additionally, we had a focus group session where we asked twenty selected people from the group to tell us what they loved about the film and what they did not like. Fifteen out of the twenty said they did not like the ending of the film. Some of them said why. Fair enough – it seemed to be a strong majority opinion. The audience, in this case the statistical representatives of the audience, is almost always right. We weren't writing *The Brothers Karamazov*, and several scholars say even Shakespeare altered his texts after he'd watched the reaction of his audience.

I am never ashamed of repeating William Goldman's quote: 'No one knows anything.' Our sample audiences thought we needed a comedy button at the end. We did some additional shooting with our stars and we added the warm, fuzzy comic ending which perfectly fit the mood at the end of the film.

And that's what you'll see if you watch the movie today.

In 2003 *Bringing Down the House* opened in about 3,000 screens around the country. We were up against a movie called *Tears of the Sun*, which starred my old friend Bruce Willis, and on Friday night, since we were expecting the two films to be neck and neck, I remember waiting for a call from the president of marketing at Disney, and lo and behold, we found that we were performing better than expected at the box office on Friday evening. Saturday morning I got another call: we were performing even better than Friday, and Sunday was the same story.

The movie opened at number 1, collecting $32 million in its first weekend. It blew Bruce Willis and the competition away. It stayed at number 1 on the charts for three weeks in a row, which is unusual (especially for a movie whose budget was approximately $32 million), and went on to gross over $130 million at the box office, just in the domestic market. I received from the Neilson Company a huge trophy which is awarded to a film that crosses the $100 million mark in the domestic market.

In the foreign markets, the movie over-performed as well. Disney and I were elated and there were huge celebrations. I'm sure MGM, who passed on the project, must have felt the pain for a long time. The residual value of a hit film is cheques that one sees for many years after the release, and I still enjoy the benefits of these.

It was certainly my biggest success to date.

STUDIOS, STARS AND MORE

OVER THE LAST DECADE, a sign that I had won notice in Hollywood was that at most of my favourite restaurants, waiters who aspired to be actors or writers would hand me a photograph or script, not to be intrusive, just eager to be a part of the Hollywood dream.

A commercial success like *Bringing Down the House* can tempt you to hang up your hat or go on an extended world cruise, but Hollywood's not like that and I certainly am not. I like the action, the pace and, let's face it, producing Hollywood movies is the coolest job in the world.

I began work on the next projects very soon. Of the films I had in development, a couple certainly stood out. In 2004 I began shooting *Walking Tall*, the remake of a movie made in the 1970s that I had always loved. We went to an actor whose real name is Duane Johnson, with the stage name of 'The Rock'. Anyone who sees him or the movie or even the poster of the movie knows why. His muscles look like they're proud to be a part of him. He was perfect and luckily he loved the script.

MGM and I decided to shoot the film in Vancouver, and it was a pleasant surprise to discover that the Rock, for all his charisma and screen presence, is one of the most unassuming and modest actors I know. When it came to promoting the finished film and we wanted our star to go out 'on the road' as it were, he was more than cooperative – he was enthusiastic. A producer has to always impress upon stars, very many of whom are busy and move on to the next project once the shoot is over, that they will be required again when the marketing and publicity for the movie goes forth.

It's perfectly understandable that an actor's concentration (and I don't mean to imply that directors, writers or producers are holier than them) and focus at any moment are on the movie they have in hand rather than the one they shot six months ago. So even though most contracts contain a clause saying that the actor agrees to cooperate in the publicity and marketing of the film, one has to strike a delicate diplomatic balance in making the requests.

Out of all the actors I've worked with, the Rock was the only one who, when I told him that we had made eight dates for TV appearances to publicize the film, asked, without any sarcasm, 'Can't we do some more?' He became our promotion machine, and he was great at it. He said 'Ashok, I've been a professional wrestler for years with the WWF and on the World Wrestling Federation channel. The promotion of my work at WWF or on screen in a feature film is in my blood, it is integral to my success.' Ah! What a pleasure to deal with a smart and savvy actor. The movie did well at the box office, and much of the success was owed to the Rock's wholehearted promotion.

2004 was also the year of *Raising Helen*. Over the years, either at my friend Alan Thicke's (the popular Canadian comedian) home or at celebrity tennis events, I'd run into director Garry Marshall, who introduced Julia Roberts to the world in *Pretty Woman*. He has been more than kind to me and though I am sure he stretched it a bit, I was extremely heart-warmed (if that's a word) by Garry's quote to *Variety*: 'I usually don't like producers breathing down my neck, but [Ashok] was very good, very professional. I felt like I could always turn to him and get some help. For a director, when you are harassed and exhausted, it's very important to have somebody you can lean on.' I can tell you, I leaned on him too.

When Disney and I had developed *Raising Helen*, we took it to Garry and he said it was right up his alley. 'I know the perfect girl to do this,' he assured me. During our drive out to see her, we talked about having met over thirty years ago at a celebrity tennis tournament, where I had mentioned to him that I really wanted to be a film producer.

The actor he was talking about, the one we went to see, was Kate Hudson, the daughter of Goldie Hawn. She was our first choice. She was lovely in the movie. She had the appearance of the all-American girl-next-door and that was what we needed, something like Goldie Hawn in *Cactus Flower*.

I still can't fathom exactly why Kate isn't more of a movie star. She got married, she got divorced, she made some wrong choices with her films, and other actresses came along – welcome to Hollywood! In *Troilus and Cressida*, possibly one of Shakespeare's less frequently enacted plays in America, Achilles is sulking in his tent. He has got absorbed in personal matters and won't enter the public arena. Ulysses goes to him to persuade him. He tells him that Time has a bag of 'oblivion' in which he dumps the reputations of those who leave the stage. 'Perseverance, my dear lord, keeps honour bright,' he says. It could be emblazoned on the gates of Hollywood, though Hollywood doesn't have many welcoming gates, but lots of exits, lit up in neon.

In late 2004 I got a call from Jeff Berg, the chairman of International Creative Management (ICM), one of the leading agencies in Los Angeles, and he said, 'You had so much success with Steve Martin in *Bringing Down the House* ... he has written a screenplay from his novel *Shopgirl* and is unable to get it made. We would love to do it with you.'

I said, 'Send it over, let me take a look.' I read the script and the book over the next few days. Steve Martin is such a talented writer, actor and producer. I was enthralled with the screenplay, and decided it was something I wanted to make.

I met Steve and the director, Anand Tucker, who was half-Indian and half-British. I took it on and decided on a budget of $20 million after discussions with my international sales and marketing team. We concluded that of this budget we had to have $10 million invested from the US. I decided to call Dick Cook who was the chairman of Disney. I told him I knew they had passed on the film but that I would like him to have a second look now that the script was further developed and we had a package which had great promise. I suggested we discuss it over lunch and he agreed. I invited Jeff Berg as well. I chose a restaurant called Ca Del Sol, frequented by top Disney executives.

I had a little plot going with Steve.

Everyone in Hollywood knew that Steve and I had, as partners in *Bringing Down the House*, made serious profits for Disney and ourselves. Steve was to walk into the restaurant forty-five minutes into the lunch, the period we both judged when the real nitty-gritty of the deal would begin to be discussed.

That's how we scripted it: he would walk in, be surprised to find us there and tell Dick and Jeff how happy he was that we were making this movie with Disney and how grateful he was that they were backing it. Steve can be charming and persuasive. We planned that he would talk about the huge success of our last partnership on *Bringing Down the House*.

So our lunch began, and after half an hour I told Dick I needed $10 million. He said what I expected: that he needed to think about it. I nodded, as though to say: no problem. I was waiting. Ten minutes later Steve Martin arrived and he said he was glad to see us over here and this and that and after five minutes he said to Dick, 'Ashok tells me we are doing *Shopgirl* together – that is so great!'

Dick was caught completely off-guard. He said, 'Of course we are, Steve.'

And suddenly *Shopgirl* was a greenlit movie.

As the shopgirl we cast Claire Danes, who stars today in the iconic show *Homeland*. She played the part to perfection.

We cast Jason Schwartzman in the third role. He got talking to me and we found out that he had seen me at his uncle's vineyard. Now I hadn't been hanging around many vineyards, so I got it. Jason was Francis Ford Copolla's nephew, and Talia Shire's son.

Another serendipitous connection came to light as we began the shoot. We had cast a girl named Brigette Wilson and I was sitting on the set one day and this guy showed up in tennis gear. He seemed familiar and I looked quizzically at him. Sometimes one doesn't recognize people out of the context in which one knows them, and as recognition dawned I felt a bit silly. It was Pete Sampras and we had cast his wife in the movie. Her name was Bridgette Wilson-Sampras and I had not put it together.

We fell into chatting about (what else?) tennis, Wimbledon and his extraordinary record there which at that time was unequalled.

The post-production of *Shopgirl* proved to be challenging. Steve Martin is an utter professional, but the novel *Shopgirl* was in part autobiographical. He had written the novel and the script, and had every right to make sure the film was a proper adaptation. The story he had written was that of a relationship between an older man and a younger woman. The movie that I wanted to make was more of a triangle – an older man, a younger woman (played to perfection by Claire Danes) and a young man, played by Jason.

Steve asked me to go over to New York and I took the cut and flew over. I went to the set of *Pink Panther* and watched him shoot. We then went back to his trailer, where he wanted me to watch fifteen minutes of cut footage on *Pink Panther*. After he wrapped, we went back to his Manhattan apartment and from 10 p.m. to 2 a.m. that night we watched and rewound and watched again the cut of *Shopgirl*. I could see he was silently riveted to it the first time and then, when he asked to see it again, he started to demonstrate his restlessness.

Basically he wanted to cut or reduce Jason Schwartzman's role. He wanted the film to be more about the older man and the young girl and their romance. I didn't want to disappoint him, so I took his objections on board and went back to LA and to the cutting room to see if there was any way we could accommodate this very personal thing that Steve wanted from the film.

Over the next six weeks, I went a few times to New York and we agreed to screen the film twice in front of an audience. I wanted to prove that if he distanced himself just a fraction from the autobiographical consideration, he would see that the film was warm and wonderful and the older guy was a complex and sympathetic character who couldn't commit to a relationship. We also added a poignant voice-over, first done by Diane Keaton as a favour to Steve, but in the final film Steve did it himself and it works like a charm.

The movie works more dramatically through the juxtaposition of the young boy's figuring out his life through his love for the girl. Finally we ended up taking out about thirty seconds of the film to shorten Jason's role. It had taken a long time and a lot of emotion to arrive at, and Steve was always a gentleman through the process. One realizes that to a writer, an autobiographical work has a particular poignancy that outsiders find difficult to appreciate or penetrate, and sometimes the only thing to do is to accommodate.

The movie opened at the top ten in the US box office. Critics across the world loved *Shopgirl*, vindicating the decision we had finally made.

For the first time, I had two movies in the top ten at the same time. There was *Shopgirl* and then there was *Dreamer*. I was looking forward to making a film that had more of a family/parent/children value to it. Perhaps subconsciously, Steve's autobiographical effort had worked its magic on me. I was watching my children grow up, and some impulse told me that the experience should be reflected in my work.

At that time, Dreamworks, which was a studio created by Steven Spielberg, Jeffrey Katzenberg and David Geffen, was trying to get *Dreamer* off the ground. It was written by a young man named John Gatins, a terrific young writer (who recently wrote *Flight* starring Denzel Washington), and was inspired by a true story, and he wanted to direct it as well. Adam Goodman, who was President of Production at Dreamworks at that time, and is currently president of Paramount Pictures, was a friend of mine. He called me up, wanting to know if I would be interested in co-producing and co-financing the picture, and he sent over the script.

I remember getting on a plane from Los Angeles to India, and reading the script on the way. I couldn't put it down. I had tears in my eyes three hours into the flight. The stewardess came up to me and said, 'Mr Amritraj, are you okay? Can I get you something or take care of anything for you?' I said, 'No, no, I'm completely fine.'

I landed in India and called up Adam, and I said this is a movie I want to make.

We partnered on it. Kurt Russell (who I knew since he has been with Goldie Hawn for many years) and the talented young actor Dakota Fanning came on board to star in the film along with five or six horses to play the role of *Dreamer*, the horse the film was named after.

To test it out before release we wanted to get away from the LA focus groups and so we went to Santa Fe, New Mexico, on David Geffen's private jet. We wanted to see what middle America thought of it. We needn't have been apprehensive – the movie tested very well.

In September of 2005, I took my family to the Toronto International Film Festival. For the first time, I believe, there were two official red-carpet screenings of one producer's movies. Dreamworks and I had Kurt Russell and Dakota Fanning there, along with John Gatins, for the premiere and party. The following day was the screening for *Shopgirl* with Steve Martin and Claire Danes in attendance, with much press attention and hoopla in classic Hollywood style.

It was for me my big fat Toronto Festival, not because I walked the red carpet twice, but mainly because Chitra and Priya and Milan were there with me and it was great to be together. We stayed at the Soho Hotel and the stars of *Shopgirl* and *Dreamer* were there, in and out of the occasions and events. Steve Martin was terrific. He came over and put his arm around Milan, and it was fun to see Claire Danes and Dakota Fanning chatting with Priya.

The kids really got into the festival environment and I like to think that perhaps they saw a different side of me. I am very sure

Milan did. When he was two or three years old, he would hear me talking about the opening of one film or the other and must have on several occasions heard me mention the American Multi-Cinema (AMC) theatre chain. He had overheard me saying I was off to previews at this or that theatre and somewhere in his mind he concluded that I worked for the AMC theatres. He would tell guests with whom he struck up conversations that 'Daddy works at AMC.' I can't say what went on in his infant head – maybe he thought I showed people to their seats with a torch or sold popcorn? So at the age of seven, he was finally disabused of that notion when he accompanied me to the Toronto festival. I think he knows now what I do.

Dreamer is one of my favourites, and also a favourite of Spielberg's. It is a movie that I enjoyed taking my children to. They had come to the premieres of *Bandits* and *Bringing Down the House* and all my other films, but this was special. It won awards from the Parents Council and from various other family festivals around the world.

My children were growing up. In 2004 Milan was six years old, and Priya was ten. The thirty-fifth International Film Festival of India (IFFI) held for the first time in Goa in 2004 had a special showcase of five of my films under the title 'Spotlight on Ashok Amritraj, an Indian Success Story in Hollywood'. I was invited to fly down from Los Angeles and had a wonderful time interacting with people from the Indian film industry. I took Chitra and the kids with me and apart from the razzmatazz of the festival and the spotlight, we had a great time in Goa which, with its beaches, backwaters and Portuguese colonial architecture, is quite unique and beautiful. At the big ceremony Chitra looked dazzling in a shocking pink sari with her beautifully crafted emeralds that set off her soft yet sharp features.

⊰❦⊱

In 2005 a young man named Freddie Windsor worked with one of our joint venture partners, Brass Hat Films (run by two talented executives, Lars Sylvest and Nick Hamson), and with Hyde Park at the Cannes Film Festival to learn the business. A few weeks later, I received a letter from Prince and Princess Michael of Kent, who invited me to join them at Wimbledon in the royal box. I later found out that Freddie was their son.

On 30 June, having got to London the previous week, I was driven to Kensington Palace and received by Prince and Princess Michael. A chauffeur-driven limousine took us to South West London, to Wimbledon, where we were greeted with much pomp and splendour and were taken up to the royal box. I watched Maria Sharapova play her centre court match, and I remembered how thirty years before I had played the Junior Finals at Wimbledon. This experience was different. Besides the splendid drinks and eats that are served in the royal box, you are given a blanket when the weather gets a little chilly and made to feel that you may have pretty much anything else you can think of. Ah ... the royal life!

Each spring since the time our children were quite young, we made a family date to travel to different parts of the world, and for two weeks, my business was relegated to two hours a day. Deals with stars and directors were put on hold, depending on gondola trips or bicycle rides.

Over the years it has been an honour to receive various awards from India, including 'Producer of the Decade' and 'Extraordinary

Contribution by an Indian to International Cinema', and in Hollywood, 'The Producer of Vision' and recognitions from the United States Congress, amongst others. The awards took kind notice of my efforts over the past decades to bridge the two worlds together.

By late 2006 Hyde Park was presented with more projects than ever before, but I was searching for something different, the kind of movie I hadn't tackled previously.

A writer named Bill Kelly and his agent Tom Strickler, who was a partner at Endeavour (today it is William Morris Endeavour, after its merger with the William Morris Agency), called me and came over to the office. Bill brought along his script, *Premonition*. He told me he had developed the screenplay at Sony and they had passed on it and put it into turnaround, which meant that it could be purchased from the studio if another studio or producer wished to make it, especially one that they liked.

Premonition, as many colleagues have said, is reminiscent of an Indian thriller. But they said the same thing about *Double Impact* and *Raising Helen* and *Bringing Down the House* and so many of my other successful films. *Premonition* was an original script in which a woman lives her life in days out of order. For example, the movie starts on a Saturday, goes back to a Monday, moves forward to a Friday and so on, with her trying to figure out and piece her life together and fix the catastrophic events that, with her glimpse into the future, she knows are about to occur. It was a very smart script, but it would take a gifted and very intuitive actress to play the role.

My first step was to take it to my friends Jeff Blake and Valerie Van Galder, who were running distribution and marketing at Columbia Pictures. My offer to them was that I would fully finance the film if they would distribute it in the US and Canada and put up $35 million in prints and advertising dollars to open the film on 2,800 screens in North America. They agreed.

The first actor who came to mind and whom I approached was Sandra Bullock. Sandy had been known for comedy, with movies like *Two Weeks Notice* and *Miss Congeniality*. She was one of the most popular actors in Hollywood. I consider myself extremely lucky that she liked the script. She said it was different and would get her out of comedy and demonstrate a different dimension of her acting talents.

We had some good meetings at her office off Sunset Boulevard where her successful production company is housed. Her script notes and comments were precise and well thought out. We made a deal and together we set out looking for a young, talented director not spoiled by the studio system, where budgets and personalities tend to spin out of control.

We found a German director called Mennan Yapo who had made one German film previously, which both Sandy and I liked. I flew him into LA from Munich and the three of us had a series of great meetings. Sandy had spent fourteen years of her early life in Germany, and spoke fluent German. They got along famously.

The budget for the film was an extremely reasonable $20 million, and Sandy, who had received $17 million for her last comedy, agreed to defer a majority of her salary and become my partner on the film.

We shot *Premonition* in Shreveport, Louisiana, a small town where there is really nothing to do, but fitted the location perfectly for the film. It was a tough shoot as I soon realized, because the director was having a difficult time translating the material to the screen, but there was no turning back. I had my battles with him and spent a lot of time on the set to get what I needed. The battles continued all through post-production.

I can remember one particular episode: Although Mennan was not a member of the Directors Guild, his contract still followed Directors Guild rules, which allowed him ten weeks to put together a 'director's cut' of the film. Ten weeks passed, and at the start of the eleventh, I gave Mennan a call to let him know I wanted to see his cut of the picture. He said he wasn't yet ready to show it.

I made that same call on the twelfth and thirteenth week, and Mennan's cut was still not complete. It became apparent that not only was he not going to be ready with his cut, but that his delays would cause us to miss the delivery date to the foreign distributors, which would be absolutely disastrous. If we failed to deliver the finished film on the agreed-upon date, three things would happen: I would be in breach of contract with over a dozen distributors; all of those distributors would miss their release dates; and they would all sue me for millions of dollars.

This is definitely the trickier side of producing. I needed to see what Mennan had put together as soon as possible, but I knew that he would try to prevent me from getting a look at it before he was ready. Luckily, I had hired the assistant editor on the project, and I had a direct line to him.

On Wednesday afternoon of the fourteenth week, I called the assistant and asked him to make me a copy of the current cut. I then arranged for Mennan to meet me in the editing room. When I arrived, Mennan, his editor and the assistant editor were all present. I looked at the assistant, and with a subtle nod of the head he confirmed that he had made the copy. I asked Mennan if he had his version ready.

'As I mentioned on the phone,' Mennan said, 'my cut is not ready.'

I said, 'You're way behind schedule, and it's become a real problem. I know there is a cut, and I'd like to see it.'

Mennan wouldn't budge. We exchanged a few words, and eventually I looked at the assistant editor, who had burned the film to a disc. I said, 'Bring me the cut.'

You might think that the mental toughness I'd developed on the tennis court would be the only trait from those days that I'd need in Hollywood. Not true. There, in the *Premonition* cutting room, I had to use my physical agility once more when Mennan made a grab for the disc. If another person had walked into the room at that moment, what would they have thought? Two grown men playing a game of tug o' war with a multi-million dollar movie! But I was quicker, and I pushed him aside as he followed me to the door trying to block my way. We had a scuffle and more words, but at the end of the day, I had the disc in my hand, and drove back to my office.

Needless to say, the cut was not what I wanted, and we had a variety of meetings thereafter, both with the studio (Sony Pictures) as well as with Sandy. The final cut of the picture was a combination of Sony's, Sandy Bullock's and my comments, and that is what we see in the theatres today. It was a difficult experience with many lessons learned, but the end product was terrific, and the distributors got their delivery in the nick of time in order to make their release dates. The picture went on to become a tremendous success, opening at number two and grossing over $84 million worldwide.

Sandy, who was a complete professional throughout the production, was now universally seen as more than a comedy star, and set the stage for her next dramatic turn in *The Blind Side*, for which she won an Oscar.

At the 2011 Berlin Film Festival, I saw Mennan across the room. As I was about to turn away, he rushed over, pulled me into a hug and asked, 'How's the chief?' Go, figure!

In 2005, sadly, MGM was sold to a group of investors who were not quite sure what to do with it, and eventually destroyed MGM forever. Today it is a pale shadow of what it once was, and is no longer a studio.

I terminated my deal with MGM on a first-look, kept my second-look deal with Disney, but decided to replace my first-look and moved from MGM into a deal with 20th Century Fox. From 2005 onwards, I had a four-year deal with 20th Century Fox as my first-look.

Incidentally, my lawyer Skip Brittenham represented the two co-chairmen of 20th Century Fox, Jim Gianopulos and Tom Rothman. I went to see Jim, who was an old friend, and Tom Rothman, who had played in my charity tennis events at the Riviera country club, and sat down and told them the kind of movies I was making and intended to make. They were very familiar with my career and said, 'We would love to have you here at Fox.' We started to talk about the details; Skip was of course negotiating my deal and, in a way, negotiating 20th Century Fox's deal as well.

At this time, the most important Oscar party was the one which Ed Limato, one of Hollywood's most influential agents, threw. Ed represented Steve Martin, Denzel Washington, Mel Gibson and many others and was known as a great host. It was the night before the Oscars, and every major industry player who was lucky enough to be invited would be there. Chitra and I had been going to Ed's party since 2000. In March 2005 we bumped into Jim and Tom at the party. We huddled in a corner, and they said, 'We absolutely want you at Fox. We know the negotiations have taken a few months, but we will close.' The following week, the deal with Fox was closed and in the summer of 2005, I started my first-look deal with 20th Century Fox.

I had now worked with pretty much every studio in Hollywood, from the early days at Universal and 20th Century Fox, where I had development deals, to Sony Pictures, the Walt Disney Company, MGM, Warner Brothers, and now back at Fox under a four-year deal. I'm not sure how many producers in Hollywood, and certainly none in India or Asia, have worked and partnered with every major studio in Hollywood. To me it certainly has been a great thrill to do so.

MY WORLD CHANGES

23 DECEMBER 2009. IT was a rare evening for me in my hometown. As the sun set, there I was with my parents, my brothers, my wife and my children along with very special guests at the poolside of the Park Hotel.

They had all gathered to celebrate the completion of my hundred films in Hollywood. *Street Fighter*, with its array of East/West talent, was the perfect film to fulfil and mark this occasion.

India's renowned film-maker Mani Ratnam spoke first, saying that in a span of few decades he had seen my transition from winning tennis games to making a hundred films in Hollywood. Representing the Mumbai film industry, Subhash Ghai added that over the years he had coined a term for me – 'India's ambassador to Hollywood'. Gulshan Grover, a consummate actor, commented that every Indian actor who visited LA wanted to meet me. It was a grand event and even though I fought off sentiment, tears came to my eyes.

It wasn't entirely the event. It was the sight of the frailty of my parents and, like some movie of the mind, the images of those younger, carefree days at our first home in Marina del Rey in Los Angeles and our first trip together to Europe that flashed on the screen of memory. Time ... paths to glory ... paths to decay? God, what am I? I am at best a film-maker, not a philosopher. That was the prevailing thought that evening even behind the accepting smile.

A week later, we celebrated my parents' sixtieth wedding anniversary in Chennai at … where else but the Madras Club? With all the sons, wives and grandkids along with about 150 well-wishers and relatives, many of whom I was seeing for the first time after my wedding.

The vision of my father's frailty stayed with me. It begged questions. What was the journey worth? What was real? I had given a considerable part of my life to film, to that great artistic illusion of narrative and changing emotion.

Though it passed, it wasn't a mood. I spoke to Chitra about it – several times. There would be things to do, we decided, after the whirl of Hollywood – something else. These ambitions are born and borne in mind but shelved.

The moment is seductive.

There were now celebrations for my hundred film marker in London given by the British Producers Guild, and another one in Los Angeles attended by studio chiefs, agency heads and stars both Hollywood and Indian, which was also quite spectacular, and finally as a culmination, at the Cannes Film Festival in May 2010.

Over the last decade, Hyde Park has become a major presence at Cannes. Besides the yacht parties and beach soirees, our offices are at the famed Carlton Hotel in the 'Roman Polanski suite' overlooking the Croisette and the Mediterranean. Each year before I go there, one of my office staff tips the maitre d' at the key restaurants and on the Carlton Terrace so that the best tables are always reserved for me – a practice that continues to this day. (A far cry from those early days when I would worry about the ridiculous price of a coffee at $13 or a hamburger at $40.)

Our annual yacht party routine is quite an experience. It starts with cocktails on the deck, followed by dinner with the stunning view of Cannes in the background – an extraordinary setting for business and for closing deals. I can vouch for it having worked. In some cases, we even topped off the evening with a fashion show on a ramp built on the deck. This went on for many years, until I moved the party to the Carlton Beach.

Each time I sit at the Carlton Terrace in Cannes, I remember that fateful day when a young Jean Claude Van Damme came across and re-introduced himself, and the events that led to *Double Impact*.

And it was in Cannes that my hundredth film celebrations happened. *Variety* magazine dedicated an issue to my thirty-year, hundred-film career and honoured me with a magnificent party on the beach, a beautiful tent with a cordoned-off VIP section and a dance floor, sponsored by Martini and Rossi, with plasma TVs all over showing clips of my films.

It was attended by various luminaries from the heads of studios to movie stars, including my old friend Jean Claude Van Damme who flew in with Gladys, his wife, and his family. My dear friend Barbara Broccoli who produces the James Bond films came with her daughter Angelica from London. Subhash Ghai, Shekhar Kapur – director of the award-winning *Elizabeth* – and many more were there. Chitra and the kids could not come due to the kids' final exams at the time and so, despite my exhilaration, the celebration felt incomplete.

The globe-trotting commitments and the fact of our parents still being in India, while work and school were in LA, meant that sometimes for a period of time either my wife or I would be left alone with the kids. In most cases, of course, it was my wife who stayed with the children while I travelled.

In the past six or seven years, however, Chitra has been going to India once a year without the kids in order to visit her parents as they get older. The children and I spend those ten days or two weeks quite happily together and the routine now is that we order most of the food from our favourite restaurants and have it delivered.

Even so, one particular day we decided we wanted to make pancakes for breakfast. This was not really the best move. Priya's a good cook. However, we were being a bit too optimistic in thinking we could make pancakes from scratch. The mix conglomerated in a smoky mess in the pan and before we knew it, the fire alarms of the house went off. One alarm triggered another. Pandemonium. Never throw water on burning oil if you don't want more smoke and fire alarms! All praise to the Los Angeles Fire Department whom we didn't need to call, but were reassuringly there in no time! A flattening experience.

❧

As a business, Hollywood since 2010 has been forward-looking and going global like never before. Hyde Park and I had already chartered our course in that direction over the past decades.

Continuing my passion for connecting the East and West, on one of my trips to India in 2007, over a conversation with Sunder Aaron, a dynamic executive of Sony TV India, we planned a twelve-hour TV series called *Gateway to Hollywood*.

It was a competition for viewers who had any interest in Hollywood films. The competitors had to submit a three-minute short film and they had to be those who hadn't directed previously. The competition and our show drew thousands of entries. Out of these Sony chose a list of fifty. We then invited two prominent and talented Indian directors, Ketan Mehta and Anurag Kashyap, to bring it down to a shortlist, and they chose sixteen finalists.

The channel had announced and publicized the competition for a while but our on-air twelve hours began with the shortlist. We sketched out how we had arrived at the shortlist in classic showbiz fashion and then I came on as the gatekeeper to the gateway to Hollywood. I had two co-hosts, the talented director Anurag Basu and the actor Rajat Kapoor who has since become a successful director as well.

The contestants were given various tasks: to pitch a story, do storyboards, shoot a scene, and make short films. With each test, contestants were eliminated. Then, in reality-competition style, we added a guest star from amongst prominent Bollywood personalities. So in one episode we had the director Mahesh Bhatt and in another, the prize-winning cameraman Santosh Sivan who had made the film *The Terrorist*.

In each episode, I also invited my director friends from Hollywood to give advice and golden tips to the participants. I had Randy Wallace who wrote *Braveheart*, Jon Turteltaub who directed *National Treasure* and Brad Silberling, and others.

The whole show was shot in Mumbai at Whistling Woods, Subhash Ghai's film school, on a specially built set, and transmitted on Sony's Pix channel. Sony screens classic English films under the aegis of this company.

The winner, Bejoy Nambiar, came to LA, spent six weeks at Hyde Park and developed a script with us, which he later directed in Hindi. He is a talented young man, and I believe he will go on to a successful career.

As I look back, connecting the dots between the East and

West has been very satisfying and my early pioneering efforts have certainly borne fruit.

Though I am not a part of it, I certainly consider the Indian fraternity of the big screen my colleagues. I have friends there who visit me in Hollywood and whom I see when I am in India. I have known the veteran directors Yash Chopra (such a great loss to the film industry when he passed away unexpectedly) and Subhash Ghai for years, and apart from spending time with Subhash at Cannes and at other international events, he has visited me several times in LA and he invariably throws a party for me when I am in Mumbai.

It was at one of these parties, nearly twenty years ago, that I first met Shahrukh Khan, a superstar of the Indian screen. He was a star even then but has certainly attained extraordinary stature today, besides being one of the hardest working actors in Bollywood. Exchanging stories in his trailer one afternoon during the LA shoot of *My Name Is Khan*, we discussed everything from his and my upcoming films to the surgery on his neck and my back problems. In December 2005 it was a pleasure to host a celebrity party for him in LA as his film *Paheli* had been chosen as India's entry that year for the Foreign Film Oscar.

A director and producer of multiple Indian hit films is Karan Johar, who I have enjoyed spending time with over the years. He is equally familiar with Eastern and Western conventions of art and manner and apart from being a film-maker, has been a charming and very popular talk show host. For me he is a raconteur extraordinaire and can captivate a dinner party with his recollections and stories which are replete with funny, irreverent imitations of voices and expressions.

The one film that did make it from India to the Oscar

nominations for Best Foreign Film and one that has received kudos at various film festivals was Aamir Khan's *Lagaan*. Aamir – another superstar of the Indian screen, who has for decades played the most exacting roles, now turned producer of innovative and inventive Indian films – along with his director Ashutosh Gowarikar called me when they were putting their film together. Two years later, when it was made and nominated for the Foreign Film Oscar, they visited me at my MGM office and we spent a very enjoyable afternoon talking and discussing cinema.

During the Cannes Film Festival, it has also been most enjoyable to host, at my Carlton Hotel suite, talents such as Vidhu Vinod Chopra and his lovely wife Anupama, Rakeysh Mehra, Preity Zinta, Shekhar Kapur and many more. Other directors, actors and producers, among them Mani Ratnam, Anil Kapoor, Kamal Hassan and his talented family, Gulshan Grover, A.R. Rahman, Manmohan Shetty, entrepreneur extraordinaire of Indian cinema, and a host of others have either dropped by my office or come to my home in LA for a meal where we talk about everything under the sun – from films, the parallel industries, the ups, the downs, the laughs, the tears, to world politics. Taking a role call of the Indian talent I have encountered, it is no wonder that Indian cinema has grown and prospered internationally.

Apart from my connections in Bollywood, I have remained associated with other aspects of India. On one of our regular pilgrimages to the Velankanni Church, I met with the parish priest and having listened to his plans decided that for all the great gifts given to me and my family by the church, we would become the major donors of a 'Chapel of Reflection', a standalone structure adjacent to the main church. I sought some advice and we designed the chapel and called for local artists to present us with their ideas.

Over the months the chapel was constructed and the artists we commissioned adorned it with beautiful paintings, one of them depicting in 3D Christ carrying the cross to Calvary.

~~~

It was now our twentieth wedding anniversary and I wanted to get Chitra something special. What does one get a woman who graciously says she has everything? Through Priya and through a bit of prying I discovered that Chitra was very keen on getting a particular handbag. She enjoys her handbags and her shoes, but I think that among the two the handbag takes pride of place. I learnt that she'd really like a Birkin bag from Hermes. The Birkin bag was created in Paris by the Hermes CEO, Jean-Louis Dumas, for the English actor and singer Jane Birkin after the two had met and talked on a plane. Little did I know the bag is famous for being impossible to find. Call me naïve but I thought to myself: how tough can it be to get Chitra a Birkin bag? She really wants it.

So I went over to Beverly Hills, to the Hermes store, and they told me it would be a two-year wait. I said that wouldn't do, our anniversary was in a few weeks. I got to the Cannes Film Festival, and every day sent one of my staff to the Hermes store to check if there was a Birkin bag. Finally, one Birkin bag showed up and the guy from the store called me and said, 'We've got a Birkin bag! But there are quite a few customers here wanting it.' I told him to hold on to it. I left the Russian buyer of my film in my office with the rest of my staff and ran down the street to the Hermes store, and said, 'Listen, this is for my twentieth anniversary.' The guy said, 'Come down the side entrance,' which I did. I paid for it right there, an exorbitant price of over 10,000 Euro (about $13,000). Note that it's not made of gold! The guy wrapped it and gave it to me.

Now the bag and the wrapping were so large that I couldn't check them in and I knew Chitra would kill me if it got damaged, so I carried it through customs at the Nice airport and the London airport where I changed planes, and finally at the LA airport, where the lady at customs looked at it and asked, 'What's that?'

'It's a Birkin bag,' I said.

'You got a Birkin bag? That's unbelievable! Go right through,' she said, sparing me the 40 per cent duty.

It's something that I am not going to do again in a hurry – perhaps on our fiftieth anniversary ... but will women still carry bags then?

~⊙~

In 2007 I was spending quite a lot of time in Singapore, and the Media Development Authority (MDA) there, which is the media arm of the government, approached me to see if Hyde Park would like to base its Asian headquarters in Singapore. I had also been approached by the Chinese and the South Koreans to see if Hyde Park would want to situate there. I chose Singapore. It is the perfect gateway between the East and the West and a country where copyright law is well protected. A combination of that, along with the keenness and great attitude of the MDA towards encouraging young film-makers, helped my decision. In late 2008, the HP/MDA deal was announced.

In May of 2008, on the way from London to the Cannes Film Festival, a very tall, lanky American guy who looked vaguely familiar approached me. He stuck his hand out and introduced himself, 'Ashok, I'm Ed Borgerding.' I recalled meeting him at the

Walt Disney Company where he used to work in the international television division and where I had a motion picture deal. He said that he had been made the CEO of the Abu Dhabi Media Company (ADMC).

'What's that?' I asked.

'We are one of the largest media companies in the Middle East. We are considering investing in Hollywood.'

It seemed like a reasonably good time to bring up the fact that Hyde Park was a very successful Hollywood company. He was well aware of my track record, and we struck up a conversation about the possibility of Hyde Park and ADMC doing a joint venture.

The Hyde Park-Image Nation (Image Nation was the name given to the subsidary of ADMC investing in motion pictures) relationship started out of a purely coincidental plane flight from London to Nice.

The conversations progressed quickly. My lawyers in LA and about five lawyers of Image Nation were on the phone for the next six months, and by the time we came to January of 2009, Hyde Park-Image Nation Ltd was formed, a 50/50 venture with a significant contribution from Image Nation, and a multi-year, multi-million dollar agreement that was long term.

I flew to Abu Dhabi to meet my new partners. I was received by the chairman of ADMC, Mohamed al Mazrouei, and Ed Borgerding. I was invited to dinner at Mohamed's house, so there we were, seated on the ground, and eating lamb biryani with our hands. It was almost like being in India. After dinner Mohamed proposed that we go back to his tent. I thought to myself, 'Oh, not the tent, because my back is not too great in tents.' We went back to his tent. I had my back pillow with me (I had taken to carrying a back pillow and wearing tennis shoes to every meeting in whichever part of the world for comfort). It had the most lavish couches and Persian rugs, plasma TVs showing Roger Federer playing and people smoking hookahs and drinking hot tea. I called Chitra in LA on my cell phone and said, 'Darling, I think we're gonna have to put a tent next to our tennis court in the backyard.'

As I write this book, Ed Borgerding is no longer with ADMC or Image Nation and from what I understand, Mohamed has moved over to the cultural and heritage side of Abu Dhabi.

Michael Garin, an experienced executive in both the motion picture and television business, is now CEO of Image Nation and runs the company with the new chairman, Mohamed Khalifa Al Mubarak, who is in his thirties and is a huge fan of films, old and new. His grasp of story and the volume of films from Hollywood, Asia and India that he has watched is absolutely amazing. The Hyde Park-Image Nation relationship has blossomed into various successful films, and Mohamed and Michael have become my good friends.

The next step was to connect the worlds, the worlds I lived in. I introduced Image Nation and the MDA, and in addition to the Hyde Park-Image Nation relationship which was formed to make Hollywood films, we started Hyde Park-Image Nation Singapore. It kicked off in 2010, with an investment from both Image Nation and MDA. It was now converted from the original Hyde Park-MDA to Hyde Park-Image Nation MDA, bringing Singapore into the investment triangle.

The object was to make movies with story content that was relevant to Asia, India, Singapore and the Middle East, but could also be sold globally. Films with a mixture of East/West talents included *Street Fighter*, the rights for which originated in Japan from the video game company Capcom. I spent three days in Tokyo with the executives of Capcom, where I competed against all the major studios who were interested in acquiring the rights to this video game to adapt into a feature film. Over the three-day period, with a lot of bowing in the Japanese tradition, much translation back and forth and gruelling negotiations over many hours each day, the Capcom executives decided to choose me over all the other suitors.

Street Fighter was shot in Thailand, had stars from both America and Asia, a stunt team from China and various members of the crew from Australia and Thailand. Hyde Park's tentacles were spreading into the areas that meant a lot to me.

At Cannes in 2010, a Spanish distributor came to my suite and said, 'Your figure is fifty feet tall and looking down at me.' A distributor from South Korea said, 'Your car nearly ran me down on the Croisette.' I put it down to poor English, but later found that my billboard advertising Singapore towered over the Croisette. Similarly, my face was plastered on the side of smart cars all over the city. This was to advertise the fact that I had chosen Singapore as my Asian base of operations.

At present, Hyde Park, with its headquarters in Los Angeles, has offices in Abu Dhabi with Image Nation, run by Jason Mirch, a smart young Hollywood executive. In Singapore the offices are managed by another talented young man, Yee Yeo Chang, who also has spent many years in New York and LA. Finally, there is my office in Chennai, which I've had since the days of *Jeans*.

The new Hyde Park global enterprise produced movies like *Death Sentence*, directed by James Wan (who is currently directing the next *Fast and the Furious*), based on a novel by Brian Garfield. Brian had also authored the novel from which my first feature film,

Fear in a Handful of Dust, was adapted. The *Death Sentence* screenplay was excellent, and I couldn't help but feel that I had come full circle: from a young producer trying to get my first film made with this author's work, to being presented with another adaptation of his work at a point when I could green light the movie on my own, almost like a studio.

Other memorable films included *Machete* – a hit through 20th Century Fox – with an amazing cast of actors including Robert de Niro and Jessica Alba, and the TV movie *Lost Christmas*, in partnership with the BBC, which went on to win my first International Emmy Award and was nominated for a British Academy (BAFTA) Award and a UK Broadcast Award.

The Double was special due to its casting process, as the Richard Gere negotiation was perhaps the last one conducted by his long-time agent and my long-time friend Ed Limato. Ed was extremely unwell at the time, and towards the end of the negotiations he was in hospital, very close to death. It was remarkable that the loyalty he had to his clients continued to his deathbed. He called from the hospital to make sure the negotiations with Gere were being concluded, and that not only was his client happy, but that I was satisfied with the result of the deal. He wished me well with the film, and the next thing I heard, he had lapsed into a coma and passed away a few days later. Ed Limato was a class act, and they don't make talented agents like him any more.

The film had its red carpet world premiere at the Abu Dhabi Film Festival, with much celebration.

Next came the global release of *Ghost Rider: Spirit of Vengeance*, the sequel to *Ghost Rider*. *Ghost Rider* started life as a Marvel comic book. Marvel is known for its hit comics – *Fantastic Four*, *Spider Man* and *Thor* amongst others. The name comes from the first illustrated comic book, the art form that combined the militant with the magical in the character of Captain Marvel. He was the guy who could fly and who made Marvel comics take off.

Ghost Rider was a partnership between Hyde Park-Image Nation and Sony. It is a movie that has played admirably in 2D as well as 3D. For major motion pictures with a fanboy following, 3D has become a way of enhancing the movie-going experience.

The movie came together in a typical Hollywood way, which is not the way any outsider would expect. My friends at Sony, who had made the first *Ghost Rider*, called me up in June 2010 to say they had this project, but that there was a slight problem. Their contract stated that they had to shoot before 13 November. They sent me the script. I read it, met the directors and decided to move on it.

We changed the shoot location from Australia to Romania and Turkey which, in my mind, suited the landscapes and atmosphere of the film better.

Nicolas Cage had played in the original film and was back in our *Ghost Rider: Spirit of Vengeance*. With him we cast a terrific British actor named Idris Elba, and an Italian actress named Violante Placido, who had starred in a hit movie with George Clooney called *The American*.

The two young directors were Mark Neveldine and Brian Taylor. Their innovative style of shooting was one of the things that attracted me to the project. They practically invented the idea of going out on roller skates, hanging on to the back of motorcycles, turning around and shooting the scene while still rolling backwards. They are completely crazy and extraordinarily talented.

The *Ghost Rider* shoot went very well, but I needed to show six minutes of the film to my distributors in Cannes – those who had bought the film as well as those who were thinking of buying the film. This was Cannes 2011. Sony does not like, nor does any studio, showing sneak peeks of six minutes of a movie, and certainly not to foreign distributors in a foreign country. It took a lot to persuade them to allow me to show a promo to sell the movie, which I was convinced would be an international hit. Yes, in this day of uploading and downloading, there is the concern of piracy in the trade on a multi-billion dollar scale and every sweat-drop of paranoia on the part of the copyright owners of any big cinematic product is justified. If the movie is a thrill, one has to own and guard the thrills.

Sony duly imposed its security regime on the showing of the promo reel, and I recall the event in order to illustrate the state of play with info-security in this early part of the twenty-first century. The theatre is to have only one entrance. We needed six people in front to police this entrance and take away the cell phones from 170 guest distributors and put them all in separate cellophane bags – the phones not the distributors, though, given the extent of security, that wouldn't be beyond imagination!

The frisked and phone-less were then allowed up to the movie theatre. Inside, we had three security personnel with night vision glasses to make sure nobody had a second cell phone. The DCP, the material on which the promo exists (the film in old talk!), that was brought to Cannes, had a coded key. It couldn't be shown without activating this pin. I had to have two people travelling from LA to Cannes, one carrying the digital master and one carrying the key, and they weren't to travel together.

Once the digital master was put into the projector, the key was turned on, but after that, having given the projector number to my friends at Sony in Los Angeles, they would need to turn on a master key there and the six minutes of the trailer would play, at the end of which they would turn the key off, rendering the DCP useless.

I welcomed the 170 distributors and introduced the film to them, pointing to the screen while telling them that there were six minutes of the sneak-peek preview coming up. Boy, was that stressful! An audience of 170 disgruntled distributors who had never before this had their cell phones taken away. We watched six incredible minutes of *Ghost Rider* which played to perfection and we sold out every territory on a pre-sale basis, except Japan, which we later sold at the American Film Market in November 2011.

Flash forward. The big day arrived. 17 February 2012, Presidents Day weekend. *Ghost Rider* opened on over 3,000 screens in the US and an equal number internationally. We faced tough competition, but the film held its ground admirably, grossing over $25 million in North America alone on the first weekend. In the international markets, which are owned by Hyde Park and Image Nation, we performed even better. It was a wonderful birthday present for me as I turned fifty-six on 22 February. The ultimate global box office was over $135 million, with a budget of $57 million, and the ancillary rights would bring in significantly more than that amount.

In November of 2011, a casual discussion with Tim Kelly, the president of the National Geographic Society, led to a much more serious meeting about the future of National Geographic Films. Coincidentally, National Geographic was also partnered with Image Nation. In a matter of a couple of months, National Geographic decided that they would close down their internal films division and all future National Geographic Films would be produced by a new partnership of National Geographic-Hyde

Park-Image Nation and the CEO of the partnership would be yours truly.

❦

Besides film-making, and over the last couple of decades, philanthropy has become an important part of my life, giving back for all the blessings bestowed on me and my family – not only to the film-making community through the Motion Picture and Television Foundation, but also through various Indian and global charities.

In 2012 I was approached by Danielle Zapotoczny, who runs the Creative Outreach Program at the United Nations, to help connect the West and the East, and to shine a spotlight on various priority issues of the UN. After discussions at the UN headquarters in New York with Assistant Secretary General Bob Orr and Deputy Secretary General Peter Launsky-Tieffenthal, we decided that I would host a six-hour show discovering documentary film-makers from the United Arab Emirates, India and Singapore, who would create short films addressing the most serious global issues that fulfilled the UN mandate. The show will film and play all over the world on different platforms in 2013, and will be a collaboration of the United Nations, *Variety* magazine, Hyde Park-Image Nation and the UCLA Burkle Center for International Relations. What a great opportunity to give back while connecting the East and West.

Looking at 2013 and beyond, with the successful global release of *Ghost Rider*, the Image Nation and MDA (Singapore) partnerships, our annual production slate of four to five films – which currently includes the Jennifer Aniston-Tim Robbins starrer *Switch*, from best-selling author Elmore Leonard; *Every Secret Thing*, starring Diane Lane and Dakota Fanning; and the family adventure *Midnight*

Sun, directed by award-winning film-maker Roger Spottiswoode
– through my Hollywood headquarters, a couple of anticipated
films through my Asian operation, and finally an acquisition of
another five to six films through Hyde Park International, Hyde
Park today is, I am happy to say, fulfilling my early ambition as a
truly global studio. It has taken my vision of connecting the East
and the West to a whole new level.

Through my years of infancy and in my teens, the connection
between the India of my childhood and the West was very tenuous.
Today, millions of people travel from India to global destinations
for work and play. My first contact with the West, which predates
this globalization by a decade and more, was through tennis and
then through my parent's inclination to visit faraway places. My
mother, unusually for an Indian lady of those times, had cultivated
an extraordinary entrepreneurial spirit and my father had risen in
his profession. Both of them had a fair sense of the West though
they were very much of the East and they imparted this to their
three boys. We shan't forget it.

And I shan't forget my father. The end of this book is dedicated
to his memory, because as I approached the final chapter, my father,
who had been ailing for some time, passed away.

On 15 November 2012, on one of my daily phone calls to my
mother, she told me that my dad had a very high temperature
and had been taken by ambulance to Chennai's most renowned
hospital, MIOT. In my mother's voice that day I detected something
I hadn't before. The ordeal of looking after my father, who had
had a touch of dementia for the past two years and was buffeted
by bouts of serious illness, was finally getting to her. Of course
no word of complaint or self-pity passed her lips.

I decided to cancel my Thanksgiving plans with my family,

jumped on a plane and was in Chennai on 19 November.

For the next week, from 20–26 November, my dad was in and out of consciousness. I was very glad to be able to speak a few words with him when he was conscious. In one particularly lucid moment, on 26 November, he said, 'You are a wonderful son. I'm so proud of you.' Then he looked at the doctors around us and said, 'This is my son. He came from America to see me.'

There are emotional moments in one's life and then there are moments such as these when one tries to be strong but the tears flow. At that point I did not realize that these would be his last words to me.

On 27 November I took my mother to visit my father, thinking he was getting better. The news was not good. My father had suffered a severe stroke and was unconscious. He never regained consciousness.

On 9 December, still unable to rest and embroiled in the turmoil of my father's coma and my mother's distress, I suffered a mosquito bite which brought me down with a severe attack of dengue. Now I was rushed to the ICU at the same hospital with a 104-degree fever, in a ward not far from where my father lay unconscious.

On 10 December, at 2 p.m., my father passed away. I was taken in a wheelchair to see him a few minutes later. My brother Vijay had come in a couple of days earlier, and Anand was due in the next day.

My father was ninety-one years old and lived an extraordinary life. I then realized that I had never lost someone I loved. For those of you who have, you can understand when I say it is a devastating feeling. It all happened so quickly. I was never to see my father again.

I was in ICU for the next ten days, and in very bad shape. All the organs in my body – kidney, liver, etc. – were affected and the platelets in my blood dropped to life-threatening levels. I was given platelet transfusions twice by single donors who remained anonymous and will have my gratitude forever.

On 18 December, while I was still in ICU, it was the day of my father's funeral mass and burial. After signing a release form for the hospital, I was driven to St. Theresa's Church, attended and spoke (I hope I was able to convey at least a portion of my devastated state of mind) at my father's funeral mass, which was beautifully orchestrated by Father Lawrence, the parish priest, along with five other priests and a wonderful choir.

I was driven back to the ICU from church and, luckily, my brothers were there to take care of all the other funeral arrangements.

I cannot imagine how my mother must have been feeling. Her husband of sixty-two years (almost sixty-three, their anniversary was on 29 December) passing away and her youngest son seriously ill. Later, my mother told me she spent many hours and days praying to Our Lady of Vaillankani and to St. Jude for my father to rest in peace and for my recovery. I have said this earlier, but it bears repeating: my mother is an extraordinary lady, who overcomes extreme adversity with faith, love and inner strength.

With my mother's prayers, other well-wishers and the great doctors at MIOT, as I write this chapter, I have been home with my mother for a couple of weeks through a quiet Christmas 2012 and the New Year of 2013. I have been asked to rest for another four to six weeks, and be tested again to make sure the dengue and the transfusions have left my body with no lasting ill-effects.

REFLECTIONS

LIVES END, STORIES DON'T. Yes, they have endings, but human ingenuity can always devise a sequel and a story can be as long as time.

Here's a fragment of a story: It was past midnight on an unusually warm day in Singapore and I was on a conference call with studio executives and talent agents in Los Angeles and my office in Abu Dhabi, concluding a film production deal to shoot in New York with a possible actor from India.

As I settled down after the long day with a glass of my favourite wine, it dawned on me that from riding pillion on Baalan's bicycle to driving on the freeways of Los Angeles in a 600-horse-power Bentley and jetting across oceans and continents, it has been an extraordinary journey. In the sixth grade, Milan was asked to pick a quote for his graduation, and he picked one of my favourites, which was a quote from Socrates: 'The unexamined life is not worth living.' My life and work have taken me to places I had only seen on a world map and friendships with heads of states and movie stars I used to see as icons.

Through instinct rather than consideration and philosophical thought I cultivated a belief in Albert Einstein's famous line: 'Imagination is more important than knowledge.' My journey in film began in India in my childhood imagination, the fascination with people and emotions brought alive on screen that touched my life and yet I knew I couldn't be a part of it. Film was the window to other voices, other rooms, other lives, other continents and finally, perhaps (though of course one doesn't realize it when one goes to see, absurdly, the same film thirty-four times!) the window to the self?

It was for me, first and foremost, magic, and those hours in the dark, a magical retreat. Somewhere through all the directions that life offered me and journeys it took me on (the most important ones being the disciplines and exhilarations of tennis and then the great adventure of love, commitment, children and family), the ambition to be as important to film as film was to me must have been born.

The possibility presented itself only as a mirage, not as anything tangible or solid when I first went to Hollywood to play tennis. Living in California made that mirage seem more and more real. The world of film-making was all around me. There were no paths to follow, no maps of how to get there, just the thickets of impossibility and the firm ambition that I would thrash my way through them.

It was a heroic ambition – the young man from Chennai becoming something in Hollywood, and the first thing I learnt was that clearing the path to that ambition was hard work and not heroism. Becoming somebody in an industry which is as exposed as Hollywood is unique.

Our industry is one that's not for the weak of heart, and in this, the major art form of the twentieth century, creativity and art interact with industry, capital and business. Making a film from the point of view of the producer which I wanted to be, learning the minutiae of scripts, of cameras, of crewing, of editing, of post-production and all the processes a film goes through, the personal skills required to handle directors, actors, agents and with it all how to raise money, how to strike deals, how to read a contract without getting ripped off and, finally, how to handle that visibility when it comes – requires single-minded focus.

My childhood in India was full of variety and experience. I grew up in a pure and hope-filled environment where my parents taught me to reach for the stars, an environment that inspired me to make compelling movies based on life's experiences.

I was never an academic front-runner, quite the contrary, but I have been a persistent student in the university of hard knocks and though my children have turned out to be academically bright and ambitious, I would recommend my way to only those thick-skinned enough to endure it. So when I count my blessings, I am grateful for having smashed a path or several paths through the very dense and self-protective thickets of an art and industry which appear, and are in reality, daunting.

All through the years of glitter (which still shines), I was aware that in Hollywood, stars, whether they are actors, directors, producers or studio executives, burn very brightly for a short period of time, and then the light can go out. Glitter and glamour are flattering but not sustaining elements. Hollywood is littered with reputations of careers and personalities that have sadly gone wrong.

When it came to the question of a partner and a family of my own, I chose to revert to tradition. It was a choice. I didn't fall into it without knowing what the alternatives were and, having chosen the structure, ways and ethics of the Indian tradition, I stayed with them. It was absolutely the right choice and I constantly thank God and my parents in my prayers for having given me this gift of happiness and complete contentment in my family. Yes, the children are American, but they are very specially Indian-Americans in the great tradition of this globalized world, an assimilated and culturally contributory part of it.

As a matter of course, living and working in Hollywood and travelling around the globe acquaints you with the ways and manners of the West, of the Middle East, of the Far East and of the layers of class and race cultures even within these. That my feet must stay firmly on the ground is something I learned from my parents.

As success came and then seemed to break its own bounds, with yachts, private jets, international citations and awards, property, offices and operations round the world and the satisfaction and applause from the films themselves, the temptation was to get overtaken by and be absorbed in it. It could have become my primary or only world. The trappings of success make you walk tall with the illusion of one's head in the clouds, but at the same time I felt grounded, brought down to earth by simple facts: my father had passed away, my mother was growing old and frail, and I owed them so much. I have to thank my parents and my upbringing for my firm sense of identity, and the very strong principles that they with their inherent Indian culture instilled in me.

In addition, envision the humility induced by the fact that one is accepting an international award or a commendation before a sincerely applauding audience while suffering the most excruciating back pain, hiding tears of agony behind smiles of acceptance.

Everyone has a family, but mine was a strong, ambitious, supportive, loving and, most importantly, an Indian and a Catholic one. And if there are end titles to this story, they include in star positions the people with whom I have worked, the people who have helped, and even those who have attempted to hinder me, as each such experience only made me stronger.

And I think – no, I am certain – that the solidity of my Indian background and my continuing contact with it over the last thirty years in Hollywood are responsible for the longevity of my career.

Then, rolling towards the final credits, in peak positions, my parents, Chitra and the kids, my brothers and, of course, Our Lady of Velankanni, without whom none of what you have read would have been possible.

It wasn't easy and I think my story owes a lot or everything to the fact that the path I took had never been taken before ...

Of course it's not THE END yet.

AWARDS AND CITATIONS

Lost Christmas (2012)

- 2013 Winner – International Emmy Kids Awards – Best TV Movie/Mini-Series
- 2013 Nominee – UK Broadcast Awards – Best Children's Programme
- 2012 Nominee – BAFTA Children's Awards – Best Children's Drama

Ghost Rider: Spirit of Vengeance (2012)

- 2012 Nominated BET Award – Best Actor, Idris Elba

Bernie (2012)

- Opening Night Selection of the 2011 Los Angeles Film Festival
- 2012 Winner – One of the National Board of Review's Top Ten Independent Films of 2012
- 2012 Winner – New York Film Critics Circle Awards – Best Supporting Actor – Matthew McConaughey, 2nd place Best Actor – Jack Black
- 2013 Winner – National Society of Film Critics Awards – Best Supporting Actor – Matthew McConaughey

- 2012 Nominees – Gotham Independent Film Awards – Best Film, Best Ensemble Performance
- 2013 Nominees – Broadcast Film Critics Association Awards – Best Comedy, Best Actor in a Comedy – Jack Black, Best Actress in a Comedy – Shirley MacLaine
- 2013 Nominee – Golden Globes – Best Performance by an Actor in a Motion Picture, Musical or Comedy – Jack Black
- 2013 Nominees – Independent Spirit Awards – Best Feature, Best Male Lead – Jack Black

- 2012 International Film Festival of India – honoured with retrospective of films and 'A Special Tribute to Ashok Amritraj', while Indian cinema celebrated a hundred years

Our Idiot Brother (2011)

- Official Selection of the 2011 Sundance Film Festival

Machete (2010)

- 2011 Won ALMA Award – Favourite Movie Actress, Drama/ Adventure – Jessica Alba
- 2011 Nominated ALMA Award – Movie
- 2011 Nominated ALMA Award – Movie Actor, Danny Trejo

Blue Valentine (2010)

- 2011 Nominated Academy Awards – Best Actress – Michelle Williams
- 2011 Nominated Broadcast Film Critics Association Award – Best Actor – Ryan Gosling, Best Actress – Michelle Williams

- 2010 Won Chicago Film Critics Association Award – Most Promising Filmmaker – Derek Cianfrance
- 2010 Nominated Chicago Film Critics Association Award – Best Actor – Ryan Gosling, Best Actress – Michelle Williams
- 2011 Won Chlotrudis Award – Best Actor – Ryan Gosling
- 2011 Nominated Golden Globes – Best Performance by an Actor in a Motion Picture – Ryan Gosling, Best Performance by an Actress in a Motion Picture – Michelle Williams
- 2010 Nominated Gotham Awards – Best Film
- 2011 Nominated Independent Spirit Award – Best Female Lead – Michelle Williams
- 2011 Nominated London Critics Circle Film Awards – Actor of the Year – Ryan Gosling
- 2011 Nominated Online Film Critics Society Awards – Best Actor – Ryan Gosling
- 2010 Nominated San Diego Film Critics Society Awards – Best Actress – Michelle Williams
- 2010 Won San Francisco Film Critics Circle – Best Actress – Michelle Williams
- 2010 Nominated Satellite Awards – Best Motion Picture Drama, Best Actress in a Motion Picture Drama – Michelle Williams, Best Actor in a Motion Picture Drama – Ryan Gosling
- 2010 Sundance Film Festival – Grand Jury Prize Nominee
- 2010 Nominated Toronto Film Critics Association Awards – Best Actress – Michelle Williams

- 2010 – Honoured by *Variety* magazine for his 100th film achievement

- 2009 – Ashok Amritraj named one of the Most Influential South Asian Executives in Media and Entertainment by Korn/Ferry International

Traitor (2008)

- 2008 Nominated Black Reel Awards – Best Actor – Don Cheadle
- 2008 Nominated Black Reel Awards – Best Breakthrough Performance – Saïd Taghmaoui
- 2008 Nominated Black Reel Awards – Best Film
- 2009 Image Awards – Outstanding Actor in a Motion Picture – Don Cheadle
- 2009 Nominated Academy of Science Fiction, Fantasy and Horror Films, USA Saturn Awards – Best Action/Adventure/Thriller Film

Premonition (2007)

- 2008 Nominated People's Choice Award – Favourite Movie Drama
- 2008 Nominated Young Artist Awards – Best Performance in a Feature Film – Supporting Young Actress – Courtney Taylor Burness

Death Sentence (2007)

- 2008 Nominated Young Artist Awards – Best Performance in a Feature Film – Supporting Young Actor – Fantasy or Drama – Jordan Garrett

Dreamer: Inspired by a True Story (2005)

- 2006 Critics' Choice Award Nominee – Best Family Film
- 2006 ESPY Awards Nominee – Best Sports Movie
- 2006 Young Artist Award Winner – Best Performance in a Feature Film, Leading Young Actress – Dakota Fanning
- Awarded the Parents Television Council 2005 Seal of Approval

Shopgirl (2005)

- 2006 Satellite Awards Nominee for Outstanding Screenplay – Steve Martin, Outstanding Actor in a Supporting Role, Comedy or Musical – Jason Schwartzman, Outstanding Actress in a Motion Picture, Comedy or Musical – Claire Danes, and Outstanding Motion Picture – Comedy or Musical
- 2006 Nominated Costume Designers Guild Awards – Excellence in Costume Design for Film – Contemporary – Nancy Steiner

- 2005 – Indian International Film Festival awarded Ashok Amritraj for his 'extraordinary contribution by an Indian in international cinema'

- 2005 – Ashok Amritraj named 'Producer of the Decade' by the Spirit of India Foundation

Raising Helen (2004)

- 2004 Nominated Teen Choice Awards – Choice Movie Actress – Comedy – Kate Hudson

Walking Tall (2004)

- 2004 Nominated Teen Choice Awards – Choice Movie Actor – Drama/Action Adventure – Dwayne Johnson
- 2004 Nominated World Stunt Awards – Best High Work – Tanoai Reed, Mike Dopud

- 2004 Ashok Amritraj received Certificate of Special Recognition from United States Congress for Outstanding and Invaluable Service to the Community.

- 2004 The Vision Awards presented the Producer of Vision Award to Amritraj for 'exceptional foresight and insight, and creative contribution to the enrichment of humankind'

- 2004 Awarded a Certificate of Special Congressional Recognition from the United States House of Representatives for Exemplary Public Service to the People of the United States of America

- 2004 The American Indian Foundation, chaired by former United States President Bill Clinton, awarded Amritraj a special award for 'Making India and Indians proud'

Bringing Down the House (2003)

- 2004 Won NAACP Image Award – Outstanding Actress in a Motion Picture – Queen Latifah
- 2004 Nominated MTV Movie Awards – Best Female Performance – Queen Latifah, Best Fight – Queen Latifah and Missi Pyle, Best Dance Sequence – Steve Martin

- 2004 Nominated BET Comedy Awards – Outstanding Box Office Movie
- 2004 Nominated BET Comedy Awards – Outstanding Lead Actress in a Box Office Movie – Queen Latifah
- 2003 BMI Film and TV Awards Winner – BMI Film Music Award – Lalo Schifrin
- 2004 Nominated Black Reel Awards – Best Actress – Queen Latifah
- 2003 Nominated Golden Trailer Awards – Best Comedy
- 2004 Nominated Kids Choice Awards, USA – Favourite Movie Actress – Queen Latifah
- 2003 Teen Choice Awards Winner – Choice Movie Actress – Queen Latifah
- 2003 Nominated Teen Choice Awards – Choice Movie – Comedy
- 2003 Nominated Teen Choice Awards – Choice Movie Breakout Star – Female – Queen Latifah
- 2003 Nominated Teen Choice Awards – Choice Movie Chemistry – Queen Latifah and Eugene Levy
- 2003 Nominated Teen Choice Awards – Choice Movie Fight/ Action Sequence
- 2003 Nominated Teen Choice Awards – Choice Movie Hissy Fit – Steve Martin

- 2003 Ashok Amritraj presented with a Commendation for Leadership and Service to the Golden State, from California Governor Gray Davis

- 2003 Neilsen/EDI presented Ashok Amritraj with the Golden Reel for Extraordinary Box Office Achievement for 'Bringing Down the House'

Moonlight Mile (2002)

- 2003 Las Vegas Film Critics Society Awards Winner – Best Supporting Actress – Susan Sarandon
- 2003 Phoenix Film Critics Society Award Nominee – Best Original Screenplay – Brad Silberling

Bandits (2001)

- 2002 Nominated AFI Awards – Featured Actor of the Year, Female – Cate Blanchett
- 2002 Nominated Golden Globe Awards – Best Performance by an Actor in a Motion Picture Musical or Comedy – Billy Bob Thornton
- 2002 Nominated Golden Globe Awards – Best Performance by an Actress in a Motion Picture Musical or Comedy – Cate Blanchett
- 2002 Nominated Screen Actors Guild Awards – Outstanding Performance by a Female Actor in a Supporting Role – Cate Blanchett
- 2002 Florida Film Critics Circle Awards Winner – Best Actor – Billy Bob Thornton
- 2002 Florida Film Critics Circle Awards Winner – Best Supporting Actress – Cate Blanchett
- 2001 National Board of Review Awards Winner – Best Actor – Billy Bob Thornton
- 2002 Nominated Phoenix Film Critics Society Awards – Best Actor in a Supporting Role – Billy Bob Thornton
- 2001 California on Location Awards Winner – Location Professional of the Year – Features – John Panzarella and Leslie Thorson

- 2002 Nominated World Trailer Awards – Best Title Sequence
- 2002 Nominated World Stunt Awards – Best Driving – Bruce Paul Barbour, Terry Jackson and Jacob Chambers

Antitrust (2001)

- 2001 Nominated Teen Choice Awards – Film Choice Actor – Ryan Phillippe
- 2001 Nominated World Soundtrack Awards – WSA Best Original Score of the Year Not Released on an Album – Don Davis
- 2001 Nominated Shanghai International Film Festival Golden Goblets – Best Director – Peter Howitt
- 2001 Nominated Shanghai International Film Festival Golden Goblets – Best Film – Peter Howitt
- 2002 Political Film Society, USA Awards – Democracy

- 2001 Ashok Amritraj presented with the Pride of India Award by the Bollywood Awards

Jeans (1998)

- India's Selection for Best Foreign Film Academy Award
- 1999 Won Filmfare Award – Tamil Film Industry – Best Music Director – A.R. Rahman

Double Impact (1991)

- 1992 Nominated MTV Movie Awards – Most Desirable Male – Jean Claude Van Damme

ACKNOWLEDGEMENTS

IN PUTTING MY LIFE story down on the page, it has become readily apparent how much admiration and gratitude I owe to those who've guided, taught, helped, healed and inspired me throughout the years: my mother, who started a life-changing journey when she bought me my first tennis racket; my father, whose character inspired stories that could fill a thousand more pages; my wife and children, whose unconditional love and patience make each precious day with them such an enjoyable adventure; my brothers, whose lives have been intertwined with mine. We have travelled the world and I am grateful for our continued closeness and their constant support.

In more recent years, during which I have been forced to face illness and mortality, my experiences could have been much more harrowing if not for the great skill and dedicated care of the doctors at Miot Hospital, especially Dr and Mrs Mohandas.

In terms of my career, the faith that Al Hill, Jr. and my brother Vijay had in me when we started Amritraj Productions and the invaluable advice my friend Sid Balkin offered me served to guide my early professional development.

In crafting this book, the wisdom and skill of Farrukh Dhondy proved to be vital. The time and effort put forth by Mike

Dougherty, Joe D'Angelo and Bhuvan Lall to aid in its writing is greatly appreciated, and I was extremely fortunate to be provided much-needed insight by my favourite critics, Alan Thicke, Rocky Lang and Lars Sylvest.

Finally, I would like to thank the team at HarperCollins India for their dedication and terrific effort in making this book the best that it could be.